Edited by Hannah Neate and Ruth Craggs

Modern Futures

Uniformbooks 2016

First published 2016
Copyright © Hannah Neate, Ruth Craggs, individual contributors
ISBN 978-1-910010-11-2

Uniformbooks
7 Hillhead Terrace, Axminster, Devon EX13 5JL
www.uniformbooks.co.uk

Trade distribution in the UK by Central Books
www.centralbooks.com

Printed and bound by T J International, Padstow, Cornwall

MODERN FUTURES

Contents

9   HANNAH NEATE & RUTH CRAGGS
Introduction

17   CHRISTINE WALL
"You'd concrete and say a wee prayer"—the South Bank Arts Complex and new notions of value in modern architecture

27   ESTHER JOHNSON
Mid-Century Modern Living

37   RICHARD BROOK
Mainstream Modern

47   MATTHEW WHITFIELD
The Suburbs Project

57   MATTHEW STEELE & ANGELA CONNELLY
Surveying Greater Manchester's Sacred Suburbs

67   ANDY LOCK, IN COLLABORATION WITH IAIN ANDERSON
The use of photography in recording the legacy of the modern movement in Britain's post-war landscapes

77   EDDY RHEAD
From Here to Modernity—Manchester Modernist Society

85   SALLY STONE
Gate 81

93   VERITY-JANE KEEFE
The Mobile Museum

103   IAN WAITES
'Spontaneous Estate Evolution'—Research/Practice interventions on a 1960s council estate

113 MICHAEL GALLAGHER
Architecture about us

119 NATALIE BRADBURY
Bubbling away in the background—William Mitchell's Harlow fountains

127 JOHN PENDLEBURY & AIDAN WHILE
Post-war social housing: conservation and regeneration

139 *Contributors*

141 *Photographic credits*

INTRODUCTION

Modern Futures

There has been a groundswell of interest in modernist architecture in recent years, particularly buildings that were conceived and constructed in the second half of the twentieth century. The status and value of such buildings has long been contentious, despite the fact that it has been possible, since the introduction of the 30-year rule in the 1980s, for such buildings to obtain statutory protection in the form of listing.

Statutory protection plays an important role in shaping the physical and visual appearance of our town and cityscapes, but this approach is increasingly being joined by other creative, critical and playful responses. Diverse individuals and groups are engaging with modernist architecture in the form of popular histories, documentaries and community projects, digital and social media, and the growing trend for 'mid-century modern' design products—from art prints to brutalist cushions. Alongside this growing popularity however, modernist architecture is increasingly under threat from demolition and regeneration. In light of these trends, *Modern Futures* asks: How are modernist buildings now valued and understood? What might conservation and heritage learn from creative responses to modernist sites? How might these influence planning and conservation in the future?

This book emerges from a desire to examine these divergent trends —of both increased popularity and of increased threat—to explore how they might be connected, and to consider how more popular and creative engagements might be used to inform the uncertain future of modernist buildings. Three overlapping themes run through the volume: *Documentation* (what methods are used to document modernist architecture and what values are uncovered in this process?); *Interventions* (how have different groups sought to celebrate or campaign for modernist buildings and what are the implications of these interventions?); and *Transformations* (what does regeneration and reuse mean for modernist architecture?).

Left: *St James Centre, Edinburgh.*

Documentation

The sheer volume of post-war construction and the rapid rate of demolition has resulted in the documentation and recording of modernist architecture being charged with a sense of urgency. This also raises interesting questions about how to focus attention. What should be documented—successes, failures or 'iconic examples'? Within architectural conservation there are particular ways that architecture has traditionally been documented, through technical descriptions and black and white photography of deserted buildings. Buildings prioritised tend to be by famous architects and be experimental or innovative. This emphasis on the exceptional rather than the typical means that more widespread, non-spectacular building types are often overlooked, as are the everyday uses and experiences of buildings.

In order to open up different ways of describing and understanding architecture this volume features work that highlights broader methods and approaches to documenting modernist sites such as oral histories, art installations, archives and collections, digital media, as well as art photography. These different methods move beyond a focus on 'special architectural or historic interest' and highlight divergent values that are ascribed to modernist architecture. When documentation is carried out by a wider range of people, there is an opportunity to reveal broader understandings of architectural value that might feed into official policy. As discussed by Christine Wall, this could take the form of oral histories that illuminate the overlooked labour and skills of construction workers. Interviews with residents of estates, as highlighted by Esther Johnson, communicate the everyday experiences of living in an architecturally acclaimed space, where design and aesthetics serve as only a minor feature amongst more day-to-day priorities such as neighbourliness, home-making, and the harsh realities of housing policy.

In addition to methods that draw on memories, experiences and emotions, where the scale is often small and intimate, this volume also offers examples of national and regional surveys. Concerns here are with addressing widespread and taken-for-granted building typologies by looking beyond common misconceptions about the dominance of 'ugly concrete', and turning attention to places that might be easily overlooked. These include suburbs, as well individual buildings that fall outside the architectural canon, and those designed by lesser known architects or firms. Such buildings are at the heart of Richard Brook's long-term project to document, photograph and account for what he calls 'mainstream modernism'. Whilst professional bodies such as the Royal Institute of British Architects, Historic England and Historic Environment Scotland all have extensive archive collections (both photographic and written records) their coverage is not exhaustive. As seen in Matthew Whitfield's contribution, Historic England are currently attempting to broaden their knowledge of ignored English suburbs through "an intensive programme of new research and fieldwork". Matthew Steele and Angela Connelly's Sacred Suburbs project was also concerned to more fully document suburban architecture. They demonstrate the value of unofficial archives, such as those held by churches themselves, for understanding the contribution that buildings make to local communities.

There are also wider considerations that need to be given to the role of archives—from official to personal collections, both material and digital—in shaping future understandings of modernist architecture. As Andy Lock's work in collaboration with Iain Anderson reveals, photographic representations and other forms of documentation "will in many cases outlive a modern movement building itself and play a decisive role in shaping its legacy". Architectural photographs of modernist buildings work within a visual language that privileges utopian visions of stand-alone buildings, often detached from surrounding landscapes and communities. There is no doubt that photographs taken when buildings were new and pristine are integral elements in building histories and biographies. However, privileging such images runs the risk of resulting in records of fetishised artefacts, devoid of broader context and siting, and overlooking how buildings may have been adapted, transformed or inhabited.

Interventions

The volume also examines a range of different types of intervention into modernist landscapes: creative installations, public events, popular campaigns, personal projects. Although there is some emphasis here on attempts to protect buildings through conservation-planning (including through 'listing') a much stronger current in the different chapters is the desire to intervene in ways that exceed, or indeed reject, the idea of campaigning for architectural conservation. Many of the contributions instead speak of 'celebrating' modernist architecture creatively, and of attendant emotions and affective qualities: optimism, enthusiasm, positivity, playfulness, gentleness, beauty, as well as productive nostalgia. Often these ways of engaging with modernist architecture arrived out of a frustration with traditional approaches. For Eddy Rhead, the formation of the Manchester Modernist Society provided an opportunity to move away from 'negative and soul destroying' conservation campaigning. And whilst Gate 81, discussed by Sally Stone, was conceived in order to campaign for Preston Bus Station, the project aimed to "celebrate and appreciate the building", rather than to be about 'demands, demonstration and protest'.

So what might these creative forms of engagement offer? They can offer friendship and fun. They also offer space for different kinds of skills and approaches. Beyond the architectural historian, conservation officer and town planner, others such as artists, writers, film makers, community historians, coders, bloggers and enthusiasts are contributing to creative interventions. These interventions might also provide new opportunities for engaging with communities often not involved in conservation-planning or the heritage industry (those living in modernist buildings, or displaced when they are demolished or 'regenerated' for example). Verity-Jane Keefe explains how The Mobile Museum and its perambulations around Barking and Dagenham were able to engage residents, shopkeepers and council staff through activities such as an archaeological dig and *Make Your Own Model Village*. Although many of those writing here stress that they are not campaigners, these forms of engagement might offer opportunities for campaigns and contribute to the building of broader coalitions of care behind architecture as sociability, creativity and playfulness can be harnessed to keep the work of activism going.

However, as has been well documented, creative interventions are not a panacea. Whilst they can broaden the constituency of those interested in modernist architecture, those involved (leading and participating in creative interventions and campaigns) often remain stubbornly homogenous. Despite growing popularity, the project and pastime of architectural modernism remains the committed pursuit of a select and sometimes elite group. As seen by Ian Waites, the ethics of community engagement work are complex, involving longstanding relationships, trust, and an openness to different regimes of value. They might also require a humility about what might be achieved, and an acceptance that goals in a minor key are also valuable: "maybe it's enough to do things that make a nice change, rather than them having to *make* a change".

Transformations

Because creative interventions can often also be part of processes of gentrification and regeneration which transform modernist architecture, creativity cannot be uncritically celebrated as a progressive force. Transformation of modernist buildings through regeneration, privatisation and demolition are key themes running through *Modern Futures*, whether implicitly—motivating interventions and documentation—or explicitly, in discussions of the relocation of public art in Harlow, the imminent demolition of St James Centre in Edinburgh, or the regeneration of Park Hill, Sheffield and the Balfron Tower, London. In discussions over the transformation of modernist architecture, from churches to shopping centres and housing, economic value is always a dominant force. Modernist architecture can (sometimes simplistically) be seen to stand for a starkly different politics to that of the contemporary world: more collectivist and more socially progressive. As such it can offer glimpses of past utopian ideas and possible alternatives for the future. Because these buildings are often aesthetically uncompromising, they are hard to ignore. Yet modernist buildings can be clad, covered with redevelopment banners, and built onto, even if they aren't demolished; art and sculpture can be removed or relocated. In this context modernist architecture holds an ambivalent position in the contemporary town and city centre. In the case of the St James Centre, discussed by Michael Gallagher, and of Harlow, discussed by Natalie Bradbury, public and municipal space is increasingly privatised, and modernism is displaced. Though Harlow has been rebranded as a 'sculpture town', the William Mitchell artworks which were a key part of the new town's civic architecture have been relocated and can now be found attached to the walls of a supermarket and a now defunct British Home Stores.

In these cases, economic value is linked to the value of the land on which they stand; in other examples, the 'heritage premium' attached to modernist architecture drives transformations to housing tenure. John Pendlebury and Aidan While are explicit about how listing and other forms of conservation-planning are now positioned as agents of change, rather than barriers to it. So whilst the heritagisation of modernist architecture offers some forms of protection to the built structures of modernism, this is partial. Substantial change to the fabric of buildings is tolerated to meet other social and economic goals, and even when the buildings are carefully refurbished, the architecture is often decoupled from the ideology of the Welfare State that produced it.

Despite the challenges of the political economic climate, contributions to this volume show that there are alternative futures for modernist buildings. Different forms of documentation and creative intervention offer opportunities to develop more capacious understandings of value for modernist architecture. This might be through small things: opportunities to discuss the value of modernist landscapes for the everyday lives of current and past residents; celebrations of locally loved or hated buildings; creating and preserving written, visual and oral archives of buildings that are demolished. Beyond these, the volume finishes with the argument from Pendlebury and While that there are other futures available which do not involve shifting away from the original form *or* function of modernist buildings. In Newcastle, a combination of strong community infrastructure, willing local government, and the specificities of the location (in the North East of England; nearer the edge of the city) have led to the successful regeneration of the Byker estate without any substantial change in its residency or tenure. Creative forms of documentation and intervention might contribute to such successes by challenging narratives of failure, involving and building new communities of care, documenting value beyond the economic and architectural, and persuading governments and policy makers to respond to these broader understandings. Or they might not. They might just offer a nice change, or a temporary shift in perspective. Whilst the political and economic climate offer challenges for modernist architecture and the ideological projects it was often associated with in the UK, the chapters in this book offer some examples of how it might be possible to imagine, discuss, and enact new *Modern Futures* at the micro and macro scale.

Hannah Neate & Ruth Craggs

Early stages of construction on the South Bank Arts complex.

CHRISTINE WALL

"You'd concrete and say a wee prayer"—the South Bank Arts Complex and new notions of value in modern architecture

The Queen Elizabeth Hall, Purcell Room and Hayward Gallery, built between 1961–1968, were critical to the transformation of London's South Bank into a vibrant cultural centre in the post-war period. Constructed in concrete, they have for many years borne the brunt of jokes and criticism in the popular press but are now praised and appreciated by a new generation of Londoners. The architecture of the buildings making up the South Bank Arts complex is a radical departure from traditional citadels of high culture and was conceived, in the rebellious era of the 1960s, as a democratic, non-hierarchical, urban concrete system. Placed between the elegant Festival Hall and the magnificent National Theatre, both listed by Historic England, their bulk is uncompromising and ungentle and recently described as "gloriously, irresponsibly expressive" and as "a shouting, spitting punk".[1]

Despite entering a new age of appreciation after decades of denigration, the buildings, now lauded by architects and campaigners, are still not listed and protected. Put forward for listing by Historic England, and turned down by then Minister for Architecture and Heritage John Penrose in 2012, they were assessed in the usual way in terms of their architectural interest; material quality; historic interest, and group value in relation to their surroundings. These criteria have largely determined the way we look at buildings, but inevitably have a tendency to narrow not just historical research into the potential value of buildings but also the ways in which buildings are described. Documentation very rarely includes the construction process itself and so precludes a whole series of questions. The result is the exclusion of information on the construction site and its work-

Formwork on the Queen Elizabeth Hall.

ers. In many ways we know more about the social world of medieval cathedral builders than we do about those who constructed our postwar built environment.

What follows is an attempt to interpret these monumental concrete structures from a very different perspective, one arrived at from an examination of the construction labour process involved in their making. It is based on oral histories provided by the building workers themselves. These were recorded between 2010 and 2012 as part of the Leverhulme Trust funded project *Constructing Post-War Britain: building workers' stories 1950–70* led by the author.[2] The text is taken from Historic England's list entry description and followed by excerpts from workers' own accounts who were all, unless otherwise stated, former employees of the main contractor Higgs and Hill.[3]

Building the South Bank Arts Centre

The high standards of concrete construction throughout the complex are remarkable

"We did it slowly, we didn't rush it, and we carefully monitored, with torches, looking down inside the shutter as the concrete was placed in and vibrated.[4] What you had to be very careful is, with these heavy vibrators that you use internally in concrete, if it got on the face of the shutter, it would take the markings of the sawn board off, and that is what they didn't want. On an ordinary wall, on ordinary shuttering, that didn't matter so much, but we had to be very, very careful on that. And it was a slow operation."
—Glan Davies, general foreman on Queen Elizabeth Hall

"It must have been around that time that they started coming over… that crowd were on the Southbank and at that time, we'd never seen Sikhs before, like with the turbans and their beards and all the rest of it, but by God were they first-class tradesmen! And they had all their own tools that they'd brought with them. They were first-class carpenters. You couldn't believe, I mean, the antiquated tools, as they appeared to us, and how well they could manipulate them to provide the finish. It was just incredible, you had to be very precise. It wasn't the normal, you know, crash, bang, wallop kind of shuttering. The Sikhs were first-class craftsmen. And they were first-class trade unionists as well! Yes, the quality of work, well, I suppose that's why those Sikhs were employed there. Because of their skill."
—Michael Houlihan, scaffolder with subcontractor Acrow

> "Everything was levelled and done within 5mm, which is a quarter of an inch… And that is exceptional! believe me! And it caused a few problems."
> —Ted Newbery, site foreman, Hayward Gallery

The buildings are faced externally in a mixture of in-situ concrete panels with 'rip-sawn' board markings… internal finishes in the QEH [Queen Elizabeth Hall] and PR [Purcell Rooms] are generally of board-marked concrete

> "The architect's drawings arrived, and then, from the architect's drawings, which were the outline of what they wanted our own draughtsmen drew out the shutters. They went back for approval to the architects and then our workshop onsite made the shutters up… The architects designed where the walls were, they designed the cavity, they designed the pattern. But not how to do it. We had to find the way of doing it."
> —Glan Davies

> "…probably one of the most difficult contracts Higgs and Hill have ever taken on, I would have thought, in terms of a difficult build. At peak, there were over 180 shuttering carpenters on-site, all our own men, no subcontractors."
> —Rodney Bond, assistant project manager Queen Elizabeth Hall

The facetted piers and the undersides and edges of the platforms and the flanks of the minor stairs are of in-situ concrete with 'rip-sawn' board markings. The piers are related to the platforms by the flat-slab method of construction and have 'mushroom' heads

> "The first [mushroom] column we did in poured concrete, and when it was struck down, right down the bottom, about the size… well, less than the size of a dinner plate, there was a little bit of spoiling in the concrete, and that would have been below ground level at the finish, but we were made to take it down. Yeah, terrible! So, anyway, we took it down, but a lesson was well learnt…"
> —Ted Newbery, site foreman, Hayward Gallery

Features include square- and rectangular-plan towers and cantilevered balconies with solid parapets that splay outwards. The HG [Hayward Gallery], QEH [Queen Elizabeth Hall] and PR [Purcell Room] are organically related and contemporary buildings, notable for their massing…

Higgs and Hill crane.

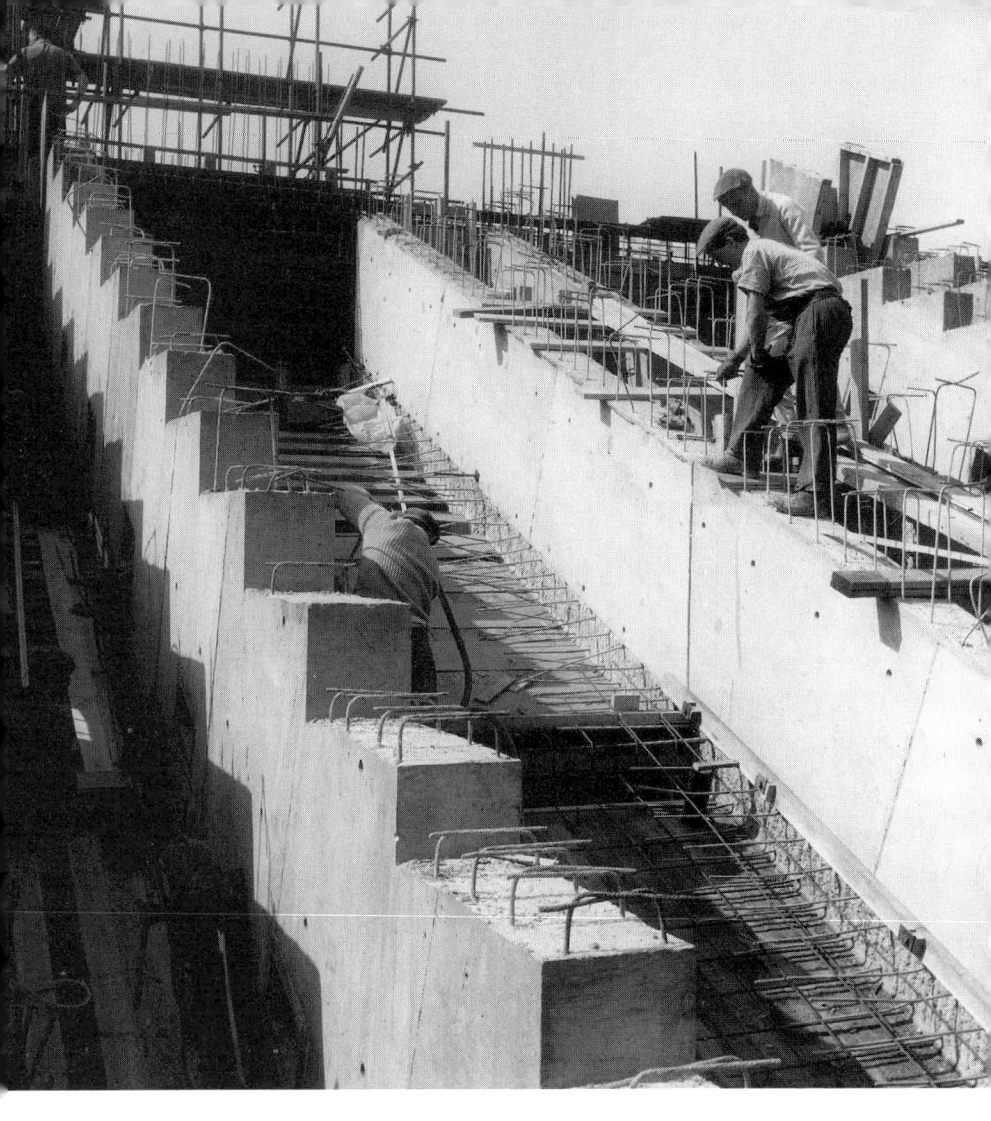

Constructing the raked seating for the Queen Elizabeth Hall.

> "Now the Queen Elizabeth Hall was a vast concrete structure, and the whole of the underside of the Queen Elizabeth Hall was built on a cantilever basis, and it was laid down and supported on some temporary steel structures, some tubular, some steel-framed, and, first of all, we built the columns up to it, and then we built the auditorium floor, which, structurally, could not support itself, and then we built the walls up from there, and eventually, we put the roof on, and it's only when the roof tied to the auditorium floor, the walls and the roof together, structurally complete, with cube results for the strength of the concrete, that we could then dismantle the supports underneath the auditorium floor."
> —Glan Davies

...the complex is significant as part of an original experiment in the methodology of British architectural design, a rare design by some of the most original architectural thinkers of the 1960s and a demonstration of their preoccupation with the informal relationship between structure, function and services...

> "It was a very happy, contented site, but a difficult site. Difficult site because…can you imagine concreting a very large wall or section of the building with all the pattern of the sawn board, and the concrete hadn't been placed properly, and you had great holes or damage to the shutter? Well, there's only one way of curing it and that's cut it all down, and the cost there would have been astronomical. It isn't something you could patch up and repair. You had to be right the first time."
> —Glan Davies

> "And when we were building it, you've got to think of the politics at the time, we thought, that in actual fact, it was being built in the manner that was for anti-nuclear blasts. In other words, there's no way a bomb could land on that thing and bring it down. It is so thick. The walls are 18 inches thick. See, I mean, it was in the time of the Cold War. When it was designed, because it was designed in the early-'60s.
>
> There's no windows in the place. And in fact, if you actually look at the actual hall, and the lead-up to the hall, they could probably close off about half a dozen doors, and they're all bloody doors about this thick, but I mean, if something really did go wrong…"
> —Graham Sargeant and Peter Day, site engineers

*

The title quote comes from Ted Newbery: "You'd concrete and say a wee prayer when you struck the shutters to make sure it was okay". It is clear from the oral histories that the key to realising the architectural specification was in the hands of the skilled workforce with the carpenters building the concrete shuttering playing a central role. Throughout the 1960s there was a shortage of skilled carpenters in the building industry but the scheme was able to make use of new sources of skilled labour that had been arriving in Britain in the immediate post-war years, for as well as Irish migration significant numbers of Caribbean and Indian workers, many of them Sikhs, entered the industry.[5] A second wave of Sikh migration from East Africa began in the mid–1960s from an established community dating from the nineteenth century when many men migrated from India to work, often as indentured labour, on railways and road building in colonial Africa, where they had gained a very positive reputation.[6] As holders of British passports many families decided to leave Kenya, Tanzania and Uganda as they prepared for independence and settle in Britain. This community of Sikhs consisted of professional and white-collar workers as well as bricklayers and carpenters who readily found work in construction.[7] By 1979 it was claimed that 40,000 Sikhs worked in the construction industry and some of these men contributed substantially to the concrete work on the South Bank Arts scheme.[8]

In 1985 the renowned architectural historian John Summerson suggested that the social world of building practice, and the ramifications of this 'world' within wider society, rather than the study of innovations in materials and structural design, should be the direction for the new discipline of construction history.[9] With the blurring of disciplinary boundaries apparent in the twenty-first century it seems only sensible that architectural history should now include the social world of building within its field of enquiry and incorporate the hitherto invisible role of the building worker.

The South Bank Arts complex is one of the last publicly funded schemes that falls within the educational program of the welfare state and was devised by a team of architects embedded within the apparatus of the London County Council. Their architectural proposal for egalitarian access to high culture was probably not understood by the men building the scheme, but it is also probable that the architects did not visit the site to explain the design to the men charged with its construction. Even if they had, building site banter would still delight in creating its own narrative, in this case conceiving a possible alternative function for the Queen Elizabeth Hall as a nuclear bunker. However, this lack of communication made no difference to the finished structure.

The designers may have been wild young men but the contractor, Higgs and Hill, was a traditional firm with a directly employed workforce. The site was a happy one, the firm benevolent towards the workforce who were recognised as part of the company and treated as such. Therefore the work was not disrupted by industrial disputes. The care with which the structure was built depended on these stable relationships and a sense of commitment to the ethos of high quality workmanship espoused by the firm. How could such a difficult, painstaking project have otherwise been completed?

This chapter, and the broader project from which it draws, demonstrates the need to include the construction process and wider, social world of the construction site in the documentation and evaluation of post-war architecture. When they are included we get a richer, more nuanced account. New valuations of architecture should recognise the labour of the construction industry's diverse workforce as intrinsically part of the buildings they produce.

---

1 Barnabas Calder, *Raw Concrete. The Beauty of Brutalism*, London: William Heinemann, 2016.

2 'Constructing Post-War Britain: Building Workers' Stories, 1950–1970', was a University of Westminster research project, funded by the Leverhulme Trust, which ran between 2010 and 2013. Its aim was to collect oral history testimonies from construction workers who were employed on five high profile sites and developments of that era. Christine Wall and Linda Clarke led the project with researchers Charlie McGuire and Olivia Muñoz Rojas. The complete recordings are archived and publically accessible at the Bishopsgate Institute, London. Pamphlets on each project are downloadable from westminster.ac.uk/probe/projects/constructing-post-war-britain. For further information contact: c.wall@westminster.ac.uk or clarkel@westminster.ac.uk

3 historicengland.org.uk/listing/the-list/list-entry/1410383 accessed 26 May 2016.

4 'Shuttering' or 'formwork' is the term used to describe the timber mould into which concrete is poured. The concrete is vibrated while still liquid to remove air bubbles and when set the formwork is taken off, or 'struck', to reveal the hardened concrete.

5 Gurharpal Singh and Darsham Singh, *Sikhs in Britain: the making of a community*, Zed Books, 2006. p.50.

6 Eleanor Nesbitt, 'Sikh Diversity in the UK: Contexts and Evolution', in Jacobsen and Myrvold eds., *Sikhs in Europe. Migration, Identities and Representations*, Farnham: Ashgate, 2011.

7 Roger Ballard, 'Differentiation and Disjunction among the Sikhs in Britain', in Barrier, N.G. and Dusenberg, V.A. eds. *The Sikh Diaspora. Migration and Experience beyond Punjab*, Chanakya Publications, 1989. p.213.

8 This figure was produced in response to the introduction of compulsory hard hats, which could not be worn on top of turbans, under new Health and Safety legislation. In the event, the government conceded to pressure from the Sikh lobby by inserting an amendment to the Employment Bill during the Committee stage in the House of Lords and Section 11 of the Employment Act (1989) recognised Sikh exemption. Gurharpal Singh, 'British Multi-Culturalism and Sikhs', *Sikh Formations: Religion, Culture, Theory*, 1:2, 2005. pp.157–173.

9 John Summerson, 'What is the history of construction?' *Construction History Journal*, vol.1, 1985. p.1.

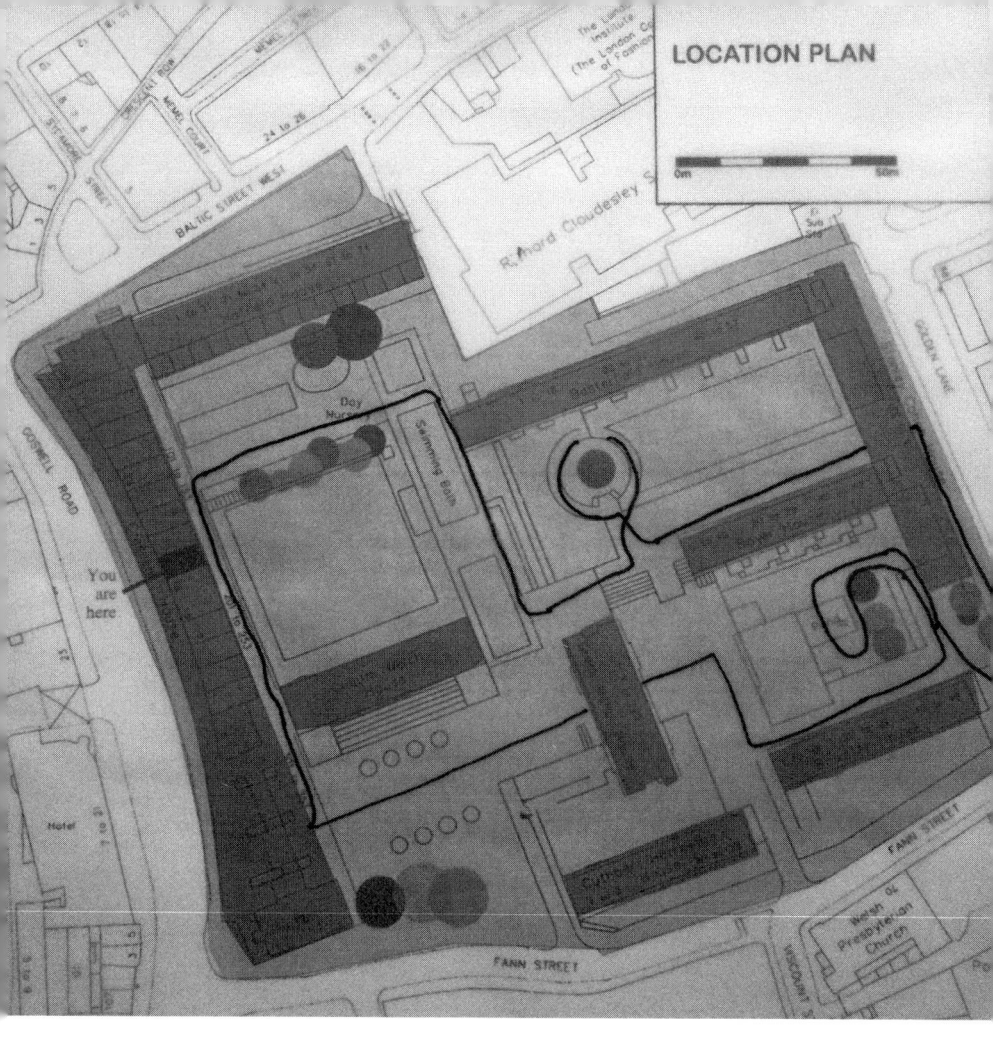

Map of Audio Walk by Pauline.

ESTHER JOHNSON

Mid-Century Modern Living

As a child I wanted to live in what I called a 'Jetson dwelling'—light, airy, and with a layout of pleasing proportions. While studying in London years later, I sought out modernist buildings during my frequent walks around the city. I imagined what it would be like to live in one of those buildings, instead of in a cramped, dark, damp flat. My walking often took me through the Golden Lane Estate in EC1. I liked not only the estate's design but also its acoustic quality—sitting on the long low-slung concrete benches, listening to the reverberations of tennis balls from the sunken court below.

Built in the late 1950s by Chamberlin, Powell and Bon, the Golden Lane estate exemplifies a utopian ideal of social housing, and is a symbol of post-war recovery. The original idea was to build council housing for the residents who serviced and worked in the blitzed City of London. From the outset, the complex was considered to be a model of social cohesion, its tenants including caretakers, cleaners, clergymen, doctors and office workers. Amenities initially included an estate office, a nursery, a police office, a pub, shops and sports facilities (a bowling green which later became tennis courts, and a swimming pool). Several of these remain. Today the estate is Grade II listed and has approximately 1,500 residents, with a split of council tenants and leaseholders.

When an opportunity came along to undertake an artist's residency on the estate, this allowed me to find out what it was actually like to live in such a pocket of calm. I lived in Cullum Welch House, and researched, photographed and recorded material for a series of residents' audio walks. For these I asked residents to record their favourite route through the estate, and to relate how it felt to them and what they noticed. Each walk exists as a sound recording with accompanying map of the route chosen. I also took a series of photographs of architectural details, and made a 45-minute film *The View From My Window Tells Me I'm Home* (2012). This is an observation and social record of Golden Lane, from the perspectives of ten residents, including short- and long-term owners and tenants.

These residents gave insights into the practicalities, quirks, and virtues of their modernist abodes, and shared memories of life on the estate, their thoughts on their own flat and its design, and talked about making a home in such an iconic and distinctive architectural environment. On the following pages are extracts from some of the oral testimonies recorded during my stay.

Photographs

p.29 *Disused Playground*
p.30 *Pool*
p.31 *Interior with plants*
p.32 *Golden Lane Estate three-dimensional cast iron signage*
p.33 *View from Stanley Cohen House*
p.34 *After hours*

Beginnings

"I've lived on the estate since December 1955. I can't remember, I think it was Chamberlain and Powell who built the place, something like that. I suppose after all these years the estate doesn't look as nice as it was… it needs a bit more paint and powder.

I came here with a lot of others that had small children and now they're all grown up and married and there's lots of us left alone and with husbands passing on, probably we think different about things.

One day we went down to King Street, which was a housing office and there we were put on a waiting list. I'd never heard of a maisonette before. It was the first time we had a bathroom because we had to share, and it was lovely to have a kitchen, and a bathroom, two bedrooms upstairs and a lounge and kitchen downstairs and we had to put a gate at the bottom of the stairs 'cos of the children.

Once we got straight we just couldn't believe it and we were so happy, oh it was really, really great, it really was."
—Doris, Stanley Cohen House

"I came in here, and it was an old lady who had suddenly died, she was in her nineties. The place was in an awful mess, the balcony was full up with coated pigeon droppings and things, it was in a hell of a state. Anyway I decided to take it, so it was all cleared out properly, and I got a guy to redecorate it and I worked on the balcony."
—Nick, Great Arthur House

"I've been living here on this estate for about three years and when I moved in I was impressed by the balcony, and the view. I think it's quite rare to see lots of sky."
—Ying, Stanley Cohen House

Home and Community

"Well, it's my home, I like the paintings, I like everything about it, I like my kitchen, I suppose my possessions, the things I've collected, what I've collected I love. For the age that these were built I think the architect did a good job. I like the garden and on a good day I'd sit out there all day if I can. I've liked it here."
—Susan, Bowater House

"I suppose it's furnished fairly traditionally, and I quite like antiques and a nice bit of art and, it's a very cosy feeling living here. Most of the people are very nice, good interaction, and it's social housing. I'm on the residents committee and the garden committee; I have an allotment, which isn't doing terribly well at the moment. And I like getting involved in that type of thing and if there are things I don't agree with I stand up and say it."
—Nick, Great Arthur House

"It's quite interesting looking at some of the flats where, obviously the owners have kind of hated the kind of modernist element and have sort

of 'pubbed' it up slightly, they've created surroundings which they feel makes it more homely."
—Chris, Bowater House

"My favourite place on the estate is above the tennis courts, on the other side, sitting on the long stone benches I guess, just watching people going by. Listening to people playing tennis, sitting there reading the newspaper."
—Pauline, Crescent House

"It's a safe estate we don't have any problems at all, we never have since we've been here. We've got a nice flat, and now that we're up here on the 14th floor it's even better, 'cos we've got no stairs to do, we don't have any problems with the lift. It is just nice. It's such a well-situated place, and they do, do lots for pensioners. You walk out of here and nine times out of ten you meet somebody and you stand and have a chat to them."
—Maureen, Great Arthur House

"The biggest difference is probably the people who live here. They are so friendly, they try to know you in person, and give you very sincere advice whenever you need it. This has not happened in the past. I lived in the Barbican [Estate] for three years and I only managed to know one neighbour very well [laughs] but here I know quite a lot of people already within three years so I'm quite happy about it. Very happy about it."
—Ying, Stanley Cohen House

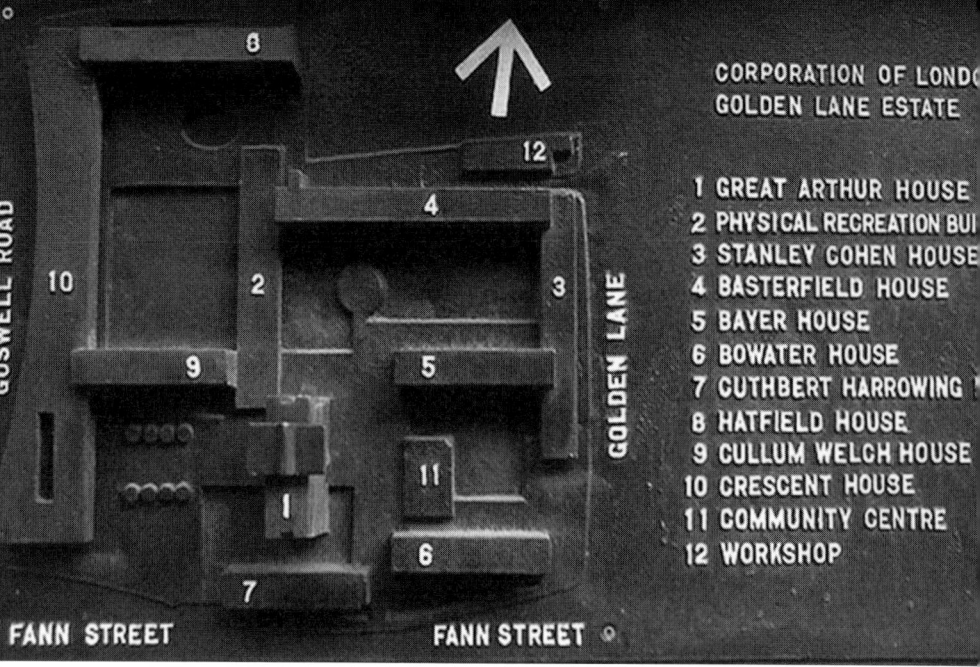

Economics

"I really don't agree with the fact that a lot of council properties have been sold off by Maggie Thatcher. A lot of people buy places and rent them out so you don't get the continuity of people who are actually corporation tenants who live here for a long time. A lot of people live here for six months, which is a great shame for social cohesion I think."
—Nick, Great Arthur House

"My son-in-law he did ask us 'cos he wanted to buy our flat, but I said, no, no I couldn't, it's just against all whatever I feel, it's against all my sort of principles I suppose.

People who'd have perhaps lived here for a long time, well all they could see was money, oh buy the flat cheap, then move out, sell it and make money or move out and let it. That's not what they were for. It changes all neighbourhoods that 'right to buy'. Where you've got a block of flats like this, you know people who've lived here for years, and you know, you get to know people and now you've got lots of strangers. They were built for working people, you can have a good job and still be earning and have a fantastic job but there are a lot of people who are not in fantastic jobs and they can't…will never be… you need porters you need cleaners, they're all doing the job, that's needing to be done."
—Maureen, Great Arthur House

Design

"I've lived in newer flats in London and, it just seems like they throw 'em up now, and there's no storage space, you don't have a sense of any kind of warmth. Here you can tell it was designed with someone living in mind.

I love the way it looks, I love the way it feels, I love the storage space I think it's fantastic, I love the sliding doors. I like the symmetry here, there's something very soothing about it.

I love the primary colours, I love the blue panels on the building across the way, looking out and seeing daily city life. I just think there was more thought put into design then, and that makes a big difference. Things were built to last then, and this flat, this estate, is a great example of that.

Great Arthur House – Big yellow, it's bold you know. It could possibly be my favourite building in London, and just being able to see that every day is fun. It just stands out, I love the, it looks like a nun's hat to me, the whatever it is on top of the tower there just looks fantastic."
—Chris, Cullum Welch House

"My least favourite building is the tower block. I don't like the colour, it's very square and long, however I love the fact that if I've been away and coming home, I can see the spaceship on the top and I'm like, I'm home, I can see where I am now.

They're all very similar but different. Next door the kitchen is where my hallway is. In this particular flat, when you come through the door there's

quite a big entranceway, which I like to call my vestibule. I think there's a lot of wasted space. I'd like to block this off somehow and have the walls go up to the ceiling, open out the kitchen, make the bathroom an en-suite bathroom and that would give me some light coming through into the bedroom.

Every few months I say to myself, I have to leave, I have to get my own place, but I'm still here 10 years later."
—Pauline, Crescent House

"I think when the estate was finished it must be very well known for the advanced design so I think it must be a very good place to live. I like the estate because I like the internal layout. Each room of this flat has at least a window from the perspective of Feng Shui it's very good, particularly from an Asian point-of-view.

Most of my neighbours are so proud of their flats. The design of the flat is definitely one of the topics that we would mention."
—Ying, Stanley Cohen House

"I mean it has got its faults. We're having the windows replaced, again a confrontation between lease-holders and tenants about the cost, but I'm on the windows and cladding committee because it really does need doing, that's one of the faults and you see that the aluminium has gone pitted and rusty and there's single glazing and they leak and its quite, cold in the winter.

I suppose things which seemed a good idea in the 50s, don't seem such

quite a good thing now but it was a very progressive thing for its time."
—Nick, Great Arthur House

"It is quite iconic. The colours represent each building and so there's obviously been quite a lot of thought on why they've chosen certain things.

The set-up and the design of the flat is really nice and it's just got little features, just the little bits and pieces that really make it unique. You notice that in the summer all the rooms are slightly shaded by the overhanging of the balcony, but in the winter when the sun's a lot lower it actually gives you more warmth in the room because you've got such big facades to the South there, that lets all the light in.

But you couldn't really have a family here I don't think. I think it's too small, maybe it's just the size of the flat that I live in, but it's kind of just more city living."
—Daniel, Basterfield House

"The thing that became apparent was that although the flats were kind of small, they were pretty well designed and in many cases much better designed as living spaces, than a lot of the Barbican flats.

I'm in a way more of a fan of the kind of brutalism of the Barbican as this kind of imposed design. This estate is probably a nicer place to live because the scale is more human and it's actually more open. I think the Barbican is much more kind of labyrinthine, and there is a kind of sense of endless corridor to it, and I think there is a sense of which people are kind of locked away. What I'm really curious about is the transition from this estate that they [Chamberlin, Powell and Bon] designed to that estate [Barbican]. This is kind of clearly based on early Corbusier. The estate here is kind of more democratic in a way because everyone kind of gets more or less the same in the sense of distance between buildings.

You kind of see how that modernist dream was supposed to function. The failure of modernism is very much one of maintenance. As a way of living, living on an estate I think it's much more congenial than living in Streatley Road NW6. It's rather like being by the sea, you know everyone likes living here. That things kind of erm, seem to work for most people. Having said that I think the woman downstairs said that, 'I can't wait to get out of this dump'!"
—Chris, Bowater House

blanchepictures.com/the-view-from-my-window-tells-me-im-home

RICHARD BROOK

Mainstream Modern

Mainstream Modern began as a photographic hobby and has developed over the last twenty years to become a full-blown project, and identity, in its own right. It is supplementary to my core academic writing, but intrinsic to its production. Here I explain how my website came to be and how my enthusiasm for the built environment of the latter half of the twentieth century became research. In this reflection I am obliged to acknowledge those who have helped and influenced my work. A number of individuals have proffered salient advice and extended arms of friendship that have been both pivotal and paramount to the roots and routes of this journey, and it would be an offence not to name them here.[1]

In 1996, armed with a cheap Samsung compact camera, loaded with my first black and white film I spent a day in Manchester shooting concrete structures. My tutor, Tom Jefferies, suggested that I should also spend some time on the dock road in Liverpool, a place with which I was familiar. I have been fascinated by infrastructure since I was a child. We lived in Lancashire, my grandmother lived near to the docks in Bootle and my paternal grandparents lived near to Leeds, which meant frequent journeys along the highly engineered M62 motorway. The bridges over the cuttings in the Pennines (see p.39) and the massive dam at Scammonden Reservoir were landmarks in my formative years.

Not long after I began taking photographs of concrete I realised that much of the built environment of the mid-century was being demolished or altered and not many appeared to care. I had some half-baked idea about making a book of the most brutal objects I could find on my travels around the north-west of England and set about making as significant photographic record as my limited skills and mobility would allow. I press ganged a friend to chauffeur me around Greater Manchester using Dennis Sharp's 1969 architectural guide to the city,

Left: *The façade of Highland House, Salford, 1996. Designed by Leach, Rhodes and Walker and completed in 1966.*

Manchester, as our map.[2] I found many buildings already vanished, including a laboratory designed by Serge Chermayeff for ICI in Blackley—which was demolished in the late 1980s. The only reference I could find to it was in Alan Powers' book.[3] It struck me that, for an émigré architect of such significance to have designed a building in Manchester and the record of it to be so scarce, there must be many more situations like it. Unfortunately, not only was it buildings of the mid-century that were, to my mind, under appreciated, it was also buildings in provincial settings that were largely ignored by scholars and interest groups, whose focus at the time seemed to be London and the south-east. Without a publisher, nor any real idea of what I was doing, I continued hunting buildings every week. Sometimes I was guided by others and sometimes I would simply happen upon something, photograph it and then do some research to find out more. It was a hobby driven by fascination, but I thought it was worthwhile.

My primary interest was the apparently un-designed. The anonymous architecture of substations, water towers, telephone exchanges, transformer stations, gasometers, pump houses and other pieces of infrastructure enthralled me as an adult as much as they had been imbibed as a child. That many of these were produced in the modernising fervour of the post-war period and aligned with my interest in the 'real' architecture of mainstream British modernism did have some personal relevance. I was also a fan of the graphics and logos of nationalised utility and transport companies and the designers of these were less anonymous. Their training was more explicitly bound in a classic mode, augmented by a drive towards new, modern forms. Now, I realise that the same was happening in architectural education in Britain, many schools were teaching the classics as students erred towards the contemporary and it was this mix of old and new, foundation and imagination, that was part of the forging of the wide, and late, adoption of modernism in Britain. I had made as many, if not more, images of functional and industrial buildings and graphics as I had conventional buildings and it was these that I first wanted to find a way to publish.

A friend, Geoff Bretherick, had just finished a Masters degree in programming at Salford University and I approached him with an idea for a website. He built me a fantastic site with a content management system that I could control, input new images and create datasets; we launched it as manctransit.co.uk in 2005 (see p.40). I was able to make sets of buildings and infrastructure like 'pedestrian transfer' and

Right: *Pedestrian bridge over the M62 along the route of the Pennine Way, 2016.*

Screen shot of website, manctransit.co.uk. Design by Geoff Bretherick.

populate them with images of subways, bridges over motorways and those odd aerial walkways that were built in tandem with elevated urban motorways—niche, but personally satisfying. It was built in Adobe Flash and can still be accessed with old machines running the Windows 98 operating system, but is otherwise digitally decaying—it's as if it has a digital half-life. I've still got the majority of the original files and could republish somewhere one day, but times move on and new projects always fill the void.

My photography of buildings within the boundary of the former Greater Manchester County continued, still without either publisher or true structure, until I received two great pieces of advice. The first came from a colleague at Building Design Partnership in Manchester, Ken Moth. Ken was a conservation architect and remains a very active member of the Victorian Society. He saw what I was up to and where my interests lay and suggested that I should join the Twentieth Century Society; I did so. The second was from a friend, Julie Fitzpatrick. Julie was teaching at Liverpool School of Architecture and forwarded an e-mail circular that advocated the virtues of grant applications to the RIBA Research Trust. I spent a few days putting mine together for an award of £5000 and it truly focussed my speculative research hobby into a deliverable project with defined limits. I was lucky enough to be one of the recipients and thus organised myself accordingly to write and format a report to reflect the research that had emerged as a product of my photographic endeavours.

Not only did the RIBA award concretise my aims, it was a defining factor in my appointment at the Manchester School of Architecture. My first full year as an academic allowed me to extend and complete a version of the project, titled *Manchester Modern: The Shape of the City*. As well as a gazetteer of 95 modern buildings I wrote 35,000 words about the genesis of the *City of Manchester Plan 1945* and why it was never realised as imagined by City Surveyor, Rowland Nicholas. I was author, proof reader, copy editor and typesetter, without any formal training in any of these skills, nor the academic networks to seek feedback and advice. Inevitably, the published volume was peppered with faults and the occasional historical inaccuracy. However, it was the first document to deal with the architecture and planning of the period in the region and led on to many more associations and projects. I made 20 hard copies in the form of a paperback A4 book, which were given to friends, family, colleagues and libraries.[4]

During the production of *Manchester Modern* I had written several short articles for magazines and websites and these began to create opportunities for collaboration as others with interest got in touch. Most significantly an enquiry by Martin Dodge from the geography department at the University of Manchester, about my work on the architecture and planning of the former UMIST campus, led to a working partnership that continues and has produced symposia, journal articles, exhibitions and walking tours. The Manchester Modernist Society also contacted me about a concrete sculptural wall on the edge of said campus that I had submitted for listing in 2008. It was one of the subjects of their early blog posts following their formation and, once we were associated, they invited me to act as an advisor to the Society. This in turn has led to innumerable events where I have been able to disseminate my research to an avid and faithful bunch of followers that the Modernist Society has galvanised in the interests of celebrating the art, architecture and culture of the twentieth century, predominantly in places that are not London. This is important to state, as the prevailing narratives of British post-war modernism tend to orientate to the capital, to the Architectural Association, to the welfare state and its Whitehall genesis and sometimes to places as far away as Hertfordshire! There are many more architectural histories outside of the south-east that have nothing to do with any of these established positions. The buildings produced were often not remarkable, almost typical. This does not mean that they are not relevant to either architectural or social and cultural history. It is often the position of post-war modern buildings as 'mainstream' that makes

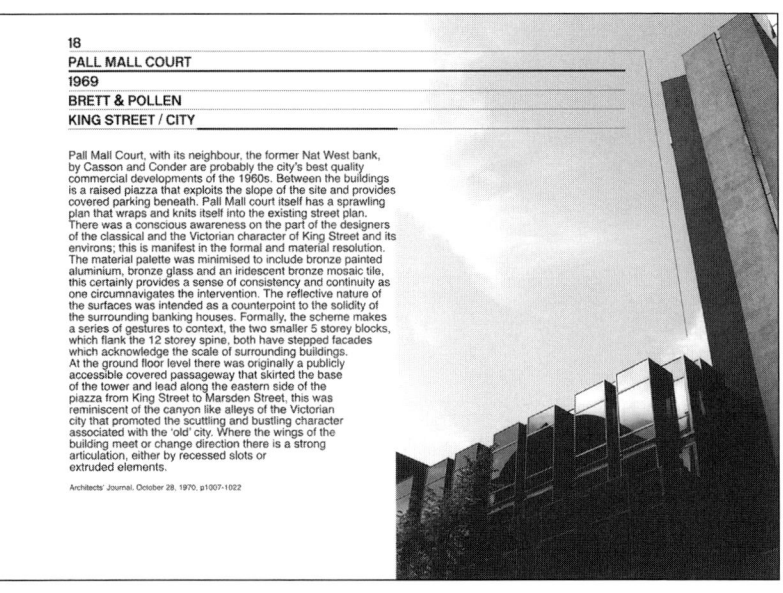

Proposed page for Manchester Modern Guide Book. Design by Vaseem Bhatti.

them easy to ignore or to denigrate—it is just this fact that makes them interesting to me. I have been lucky enough to indulge myself in writing about the logo of the GMPTE, concrete police stations and plastic classrooms in Lancashire, antenna towers of the UK microwave backbone network and other rare-groove subcomponents of mainstream modernism.[5]

The original notion of publishing a guidebook never left my mind. I know what impact Sharp's modest publication made on me and hoped to leave a similar humble but effective legacy through the activities and legwork I had put in. I have visited most of the 95 buildings in the RIBA study at least three times, once to scout and then two, or more, return visits for the right daylight conditions for photographs suitable for publication. If you add the act of photography to the journal search, recovery of articles, interviews, picture editing and writing it is easy to imagine that each building case study is four or five days of work. Multiplied by the number of buildings then it is easy to see this truly as years of production—it doesn't feel like that. One opportunity to produce the guidebook presented itself via an academic publisher and I asked my friend Vaseem Bhatti to prepare some typical layouts (see above) and a material specification. We imagined it as a field guide, like airplane spotters had, but, it was the suggestion of 111 special editions in a GRP concrete cover that made the commissioning editor baulk and it never quite came to be.[6]

Reverting to known methods, I again asked Geoff if he was willing to code a new site for me, more complex than *manctransit* and with more features and information for the reader. He'd done the same for other mutual friends and I think that the creative in him was somehow satisfied by having these challenging projects—I guess there's beauty and creativity in code too, but cannot profess to know enough to understand. The name of the site was important as I wanted it to represent this 'not London' notion and the normal, everyday and municipal aspects of the buildings I was photographing and writing about. My dad came up with a strong idea, *excapita*, which we ran with as the working title for more than a year. Eventually it was rejected as I'm not actually anti-London and have shot more than my fair share of stuff down there. *Mainstream Modern* is a bastardisation, or extension, of a term first employed by Rayner Banham to describe the wide adoption of the International Style in the 1940s and 1950s, and came about as I was reading for my PhD and in discourse with my supervisor, Professor Mark Crinson. It is an important term in my thesis and one that really captured my views and developing area of specialism. I take it to mean any built object in the modern idiom, whether of the avant-garde or a million miles away, thus absolutely delimiting the scope of my endeavour; which is as daunting as it is liberating. The website *mainstreammodern.co.uk* captures a tiny part of the work I have undertaken and is a live project that I continue to update and add to.

When commissioning the site I was clear that I not only wanted to publish photographs and archive image material, but that I also wanted to be able to geolocate the buildings, provide references and to navigate the site through different classifications: architect, year, typology and location. I wanted some visual coding of this too and the front page is a live info-graphic of just these data sets—it adjusts each time I make a new entry. I can add case studies and can host any number in a state of editing towards completion. This is not a piece of academic research in its own right, but it is a way of disseminating certain aspects to a wider public. It therefore reflects my interests: Cruickshank & Seward are very well represented because they are the major subject of my PhD thesis which explores the relationship between architecture and the state in post-war Britain. Other writings about Roger Booth, Lancashire County Architect and the under celebrated modernism of Peter Womersley have informed the visits I have made and photographs produced, and these will be my next big additions to the site. Collecting and categorising things is an endeavour that satisfies my inner nerd. I like to pretend it's somehow cool, and this has been endorsed by the rise in popularity of modernism, especially brutalism. I suspect that soon it won't be fashionable at all and the collection and I will return to a form of niche obscurity in a forgotten corner of the web. Before that happens I have managed to carve out my first virtual identity in a foray into social media as *mainstream_modern* on Instagram (opposite). It has become a portal to my main site, but has somewhat taken over in terms of the hours dedicated. The instant gratification of 200+ 'likes' from 7,500 followers is heady and addictive and it is easy to understand the popularity of the app. I have also found new information and gathered a number of interesting anecdotes from exchanges through the direct messaging function. The sense that many others appreciate the things you do is valuable too—in 1996 I felt like a loner, in itself perversely gratifying, but hard to sustain when one of the motivating factors is a sense of doing something worthwhile.

I'm not a preservationist, or a conservationist, I'm definitely a hobbyist and have been fortunate enough to follow a passion into a situation where I have been acknowledged as an expert in a particular field. Photography was my route to this journey, and naïve and unskilled as I was, I have also been lucky enough to count film maker Michael England amongst my friends and his advice about what camera I should purchase next to fulfil my aims has been invaluable. I'm not precious about what I shoot with, but it has been a rare event that I have been without a camera at any turn. I regularly used to carry a Lowe backpack with at least two cameras before the iPhone 5S was released. I now receive invitations to speak, participate in academic networks and to contribute to seminars, and journals. *Mainstream Modern* began as a passion and has evolved to become a project, sometimes peripheral to others, sometimes central to my being, that spans 20 years to date and is unlikely to wain, as my passion for architecture, be it extremely normal or extremely special, remains as it was when I pressed the shutter on the very first shot.

....

1 There are three people who don't feature by name in the narrative without whom I would have been unable to do what I do—Mum, Dad and Nina. We had about 4 holidays a year when I was young and until I was 12 they were all in the UK. I can't count how many burial mounds, stone circles, Romanesque churches, reservoirs and pillboxes we visited, but the legacy is clear.

2 Dennis Sharp, *Manchester: City Buildings Series*, London: Studio Vista, 1969.

3 Alan Powers, *Serge Chermayeff: Designer, Architect, Teacher*, London: RIBA Publications, 2001.

4 Research Award report for 2010 by Richard Brook: *Manchester Modern: the shape of the city*, 2010, 1 volume (309 p), typescript, illus. RIBA Archive ref. ReAw/Brook.

5 Richard Brook & Martin Dodge, 'Cold War Concrete: Engineering the Airwaves', *The Modernist*, 14, 2015, pp.30–33; Richard Brook, 'Police Brutality', *The Modernist*, 4, 2012, pp.12–15; Richard Brook, 'Boldly Gone', *The Modernist*, 1, 2011, pp.10–11.

6 The publication may still happen, I have not quite given it up yet.

Screen shot of mainstream_modern Instagram page.

MATTHEW WHITFIELD

The Suburbs Project

The Suburbs Project is being undertaken by research staff within Historic England with the broad aim to examine suburban development from c.1840 to the present day, defining the characteristic buildings and landscapes of suburban environments, and articulating their interest and significance. This is not specifically aimed at addressing modernist or other kinds of post-war suburb, but modern examples have been extensively assessed in line with the overall aim to improve understanding of suburban areas in the round and especially those neglected in the existing literature and protection regimes.

A synthesis of existing knowledge on the architectural and planning history of suburbs has been enhanced through an intensive programme of new research and fieldwork. The primary intention is to provide the context and understanding needed by professionals responsible for the protection and management of suburbs, but the project also sets out to boost public appreciation and awareness of everyday localities that are often taken for granted.

Suburbs are home to the majority of the population—around 80% of UK citizens live in one, by most estimates—but are rarely perceived as environments with intrinsic historic or heritage value. Although always subject to change, since the 1980s suburbs have suffered from particularly strong redevelopment pressures, whilst experiencing a steady erosion of character through incremental alteration. Previously derided or ignored, especially by architectural historians and cultural commentators, suburbia has been the object of burgeoning academic interest since the 1960s with small waves of publications addressing particular aspects of the subject.

Some protection has occurred through the designation of conservation areas by local authorities. These are most likely to include affluent spacious suburbs and pioneering or influential developments, but also centres of historic settlements overtaken by urban

Left: *The Brow, Runcorn New Town, Cheshire. Runcorn Development Corporation, 1969.*

expansion. There is nevertheless inconsistency as to the degree and spread of suburban designation. Many kinds of suburban development, especially examples of post-war modernist planning and design (and publicly built schemes even more so) remain under-appreciated and mostly unprotected. Moreover, there are areas that may not in themselves be prime candidates for conservation area status, but nonetheless have sufficient quality to warrant an effort being made to define, appreciate and enhance them.

Numerous factors threaten the character of many English suburbs, including demographic change (the effects of recent inner city and city centre regeneration, and the continued attractiveness of rural living), government policies which favour dense development on brownfield sites, including suburban gardens and landscapes, and instances of modernisation and personalisation by owner occupiers such as uPVC windows and replacement doors in historic designs. Change is inevitable and often desirable, but conservation area designation can help to manage this change in a way that preserves special features, and the broader goal of the project is to raise awareness of original design intentions in the widest range of suburban schemes which must, by definition, remain unprotected except by normal planning procedures.

Researching suburbs is challenging: the subject is vast and amorphous; there are problems of definition and typology, and academic study has historically suffered from the generally low cultural esteem in which suburbia has been held. Since the 1980s, the popularity of the subject has grown, generating a substantial body of literature across a range of academic disciplines. But the standard synthetic accounts of the historical development and architectural character of suburbs remain those published in the 1980s or earlier. Subsequent publications have tended to be studies of suburbs in particular localities rather than overviews taking a national perspective.

The state of knowledge about suburbs is inevitably patchy: while some aspects have received attention (e.g. the terraced house, garden cities and garden suburbs), others have been neglected (e.g. inter-war and post-war speculative developments, the suburban landscape and streetscape). The focus has tended towards particular suburbs (sometimes in isolation from their city or regional context), the pioneering developments (but not their successors or variants) and the initial phase of development (but not what has happened since). The tendency for architectural historians has been to focus on particular aspects of suburbia, such as the Garden City movement: studies of Letchworth Garden City, for example, turn a blind eye

Derby Place, Sheffield, South Yorkshire. Project architects: John Taylor and Peter Jackson (for Sheffield City Council Planning & Design), 1978.

Aureole Walk, Studlands Park Estate Newmarket, Suffolk. Ralph Erskine for Bovis, 1967.

to later suburban accretions following contemporary (rather than 'garden city') modernist design and planning concepts.

In this way, the suburban landscape in the round has received little attention. Despite the level of academic interest, it is questionable whether an integrated understanding of England's suburbs at a national or regional level yet exists. This can be a problem for those who have to deal with suburb-related planning issues: for example, how can the significance and character of a post-war suburb and its component buildings and landscape features be assessed when the context for judgement is often lacking?

Definitions and typologies are not easily constructed; they are mutable and possess multiple identities and boundaries. Recognising this, the initial element of the project was a development phase, to refine its scope and methodology, encompassing rapid field evaluations of selected areas of cities and towns in the Midlands, the North and the South West. It also included an assessment of the existing literature, and the commencement of a pilot study on Darlington.

Suburbs affect all of England's towns and cities and constitute a large proportion of their built environment. The timescale for understanding this impact is potentially very wide, as suburban development can be traced back to the medieval period or earlier, and substantial evidence in the form of extant buildings and road networks survives from at least the 18th century. Suburbs embrace numerous building types (houses, shops, schools, churches, garages), and the contribution of the designed landscape (roads, paths, pavements, verges, parks, greens, gardens, street furniture) to suburban character must also be considered.

The process of developing understanding has drawn on existing work by English Heritage and the former Royal Commission on the Historical Monuments of England on suburbs in particular localities. These range from the analysis of London's suburban development by the English Heritage Historians to the assessment of particular suburbs (e.g. Finsbury Park, Aldersbrook, South Acton, in London; Anfield and Breckfield, in Liverpool; Gateshead; Manningham, Bradford; Nottingham).[1] Two former English Heritage projects and publications have provided useful context: the Carscapes book and the post-war architectural survey.[2] Data generated by the Metropolitan Historic Landscape Characterisation and Extensive Urban Survey programmes has also been utilised. The resources of the Historic England Archive, particularly historic aerial photographs and relevant collections are integral to the project, in addition to new aerial photography being commissioned. Large numbers of suburban case studies have been drawn from archives of the architectural, construction and other trade press which highlights those examples considered innovative, interesting or possessing some aspect of quality at the time of their construction.

An original design for the project, based mainly on Historic Area Assessment methodology was largely (though not completely) superseded by a primarily thematic approach to the subject.[3] The project now provides an opportunity to demonstrate the symbiotic relationship that exists between thematic and geographical methodologies.

Areas visited for fieldwork were determined by identifying gaps in the existing knowledge base. A list of targets was drawn up and scrutinised to ensure that it was representative, not just geographically, but in terms of social status, economic base, period of construction and period of significant remodeling/redevelopment. Some areas have been investigated more thoroughly than others, as appropriate; others—the majority—have only resulted in a few short notes and photographs taken by Investigators. If it is evident that a visited suburb did not offer an opportunity to add to the existing knowledge base, the team moved onto the next target on their list, without an obligation to produce a report or more detailed notes. In this way, large areas have been covered to enrich the final analysis and publication.

The Suburbs Project should, at final publication stage, result in the creation of a narrative that departs from, and enriches, traditional discourses in key respects. As has been outlined, current high-level histories of suburbs and suburban development are often accounted for in terms of the idealistic, the visionary, the ground-breaking, the innovative, and the influential. They are cast in terms of models and templates. But such studies (in contrast to some local studies) rarely examine the impact of suburban visions and innovations on more ordinary suburbs, conceived, laid out and built by local authorities, local developers or national building contractors (not by visionary planners or architects of national standing) around every English town, city and, increasingly, village.

The Suburbs Project is concerned with the evolution of suburbs through time, as well as the moment of their creation. The completed book will focus on the ordinary as much as the ground-breaking. The existing historiography has been treated as a springboard for examining the phenomenon of suburban expansion in a holistic manner, questioning how iconic models were embraced (or eschewed), aped (or modified), and adapted to local conditions (or not), as their influence was rolled out across England. Establishing networks of

Manning Court, Parkside estate, Houghton Regis, Bedfordshire. Project architect: John Lawlor, 1978.

influence from place to place, and identifying mechanisms for cross-influence, is vital in constructing a national framework for the understanding of suburbs.

A national overview will be achieved by breaking the material into a number of key themes, which will develop into chapters of the monograph. These themes (presented through actual exemplars) will be conceived as separate narrative strands that weave together to produce the overview we are seeking. Each one must consider changes and adaptation, as well as new initiatives. The roles of local authorities, developers, building contractors and architects will be examined throughout as sub-themes. Themes will evolve as the writing of the book text continues, but as a starting point they can be understood as follows:

> *Models, precedents and rationale*: factors shaping urban expansion and early models of suburban development before the mid-19th century and an account of the 'suburban impulse'
>
> *Land and finance*: the range of individuals, organisations, societies and movements involved in acquiring and developing suburban schemes
>
> *Control and politics*: the planning of suburbs, the degree to which it has been controlled and the role played by ideology
>
> *Design*: examples of suburban layouts, planning approaches and stylistic treatments (particularly of residential buildings) in context
>
> *Building types*: the range of building types in suburbs with a strong focus on housing types but also sections that address the specific functions of suburbs as multi-faceted places
>
> *Landscapes*: the green spaces and designed landscapes of suburbia
>
> *Contemporary trends*: The impact of social change on suburbs (the rise in home ownership, home improvements and right-to-buy) and the conservation issues that affect suburbs

Historic England has a major statutory role to play in the formal protection of historic places, but it does not engage in the designation of conservation areas (the predominant form of protection for suburbs), and the examples explored in the project have not generated a raft of candidate buildings to be considered for listing: individual heritage assets of national significance are understandably relatively rare in suburban settings. Instead, by examining the themes detailed above on a national, comparative basis, it is hoped that both heritage sector professionals and the interested public will develop an enhanced appreciation of the ordinary places of suburbia, helping to bolster their visibility and protection in the formal planning process but also in English culture more broadly.

---

1 Andrew Saint (ed.), *London Suburbs*, London: Merrell Holberton/English Heritage, 1999.

2 Kathryn A. Morrison & John Minnis, *Carscapes: The Motor Car, Architecture, and Landscape in England*, London: Yale University Press, 2012.

3 *Understanding Place: Historic Area Assessments: Principles and Practice*, London: English Heritage, 2010.

St Barnabas, Openshaw (1961) by Leach Rhodes and Walker.

MATTHEW STEELE & ANGELA CONNELLY

Surveying Greater Manchester's Sacred Suburbs

Heading east out of Manchester in spring 2014, we caught glimpse of a small church tucked away on a side street off Ashton Old Road, Openshaw (see opposite). The windows were boarded up, detritus littered the surrounding grounds, and weeds grew up around the gravestones. A foundation stone located next to the front entrance informed us that it had been laid in 1837, and once formed part of an older church since demolished. The foundation stone was re-laid in 1961 on St Barnabas Day, commemorating the saint to whom the old church, and its replacement, was dedicated.

So why was St Barnabas abandoned after such a relatively short period? In 2005, its congregation had joined forces with that of the nearby Church of the Resurrection. When, four years later, the Church of the Resurrection was compulsorily purchased as part of the regeneration of east Manchester, the remaining church of St Barnabas was considered to be in "an out of the way location".[1] The Bishop of Manchester cautioned that keeping St Barnabas open was unsustainable, and so the parish took the opportunity to relocate to Beswick and build a new church.

The story of St Barnabas, and the reasons for its abandonment, motivated us to establish a project called *Sacred Suburbs*. We aimed to document other examples of post–1945 churches in Greater Manchester, whether thriving, abandoned, or demolished, and to tell their stories too. We wanted to go beyond traditional architectural historical narratives that emphasise the material aspects of buildings, focus too closely on the architect, and exclude the wider context behind a building's creation and subsequent use. How, for example, did the post–1945 church help connect different communities during times of urban renewal and population change? Who used these buildings, and for what purposes beyond worship? Moreover, what are the effects of declining attendance? Over the course of one year, we found around 150 examples of Christian churches across Greater Manchester, predominantly Church of England and Roman Catholic, and this number continues to grow. Here, we recount our approach to documenting the buildings and, having completed our survey, the selection criteria of examples used for an exhibition[2] and subsequent publication.[3]

Context

The target area for our research was Greater Manchester, which consists of ten local authorities and covers a large geographic area. We focussed on the Church of England, the Roman Catholic Church, and the Free Churches (or Nonconformists), who were all building significant numbers of new churches during the period concerned. Given that all three were also undergoing significant upheavals in their worshipping practices after 1945, it is important to first provide an overview of the main issues pertaining to the design of post-1945 Christian churches.

Although a departure from Gothic Revival in ecclesiastical design had begun in the interwar years, through the work of N. F. Cachemaille-Day for example, the post-1945 period is generally regarded to be architecturally innovative with respect to Christian churches in England. Yet it is only over the past decade that in-depth knowledge is accumulating around their design.[4] A number of factors prompted this innovation. First, the Churches were engaged in a process of modifying their worshipping activities: the liturgical renewal of the Roman Catholic Church's Second Vatican Council (1962–1965), for example, advocated a greater involvement of worshippers in Mass, which resulted in the re-ordering of existing church interiors and saw architects respond with radical designs for new churches. Second, new construction technologies were available that promised to drive building costs down. Third, the replanning of existing urban centres was concomitant with the building of New Towns and suburban estates which, along with an attendant population migration, required the construction of new churches closer to their potential constituents.

However, the second half of the twentieth century brought declining public participation in Christian worship, which put the continued existence of many churches in question: whereas around half of the English population attended a church on a weekly basis in the mid-nineteenth century, less than one-twelfth did so by the end of the twentieth century.[5] Since then, the decline has continued with only 4.7 per cent of the English population now regularly attending church across all denominations.[6]

The consequences of this on-going decline in mass attendance are, potentially, dramatic: for example, in late 2015, the Roman Catholic Diocese of Salford, already suffering from a lack of priests, considered the closure of around 50 per cent of its churches.[7] Although heavily represented in the UK heritage designation system, particularly in the case of the Church of England, current practice pragmatically focuses on churches which are under threat of closure or demolition, those containing the works of noted artists, and paradigmatic examples of certain architects' oeuvres. Many post-1945 churches do not meet such stringent aesthetic criteria, but are, nevertheless, of local significance and valued by their communities for their contribution to a sense of place. Protecting such buildings should be the function of the local listing system. However, the pace of urban change means that many buildings are lost before their importance is identified, locally or otherwise. This made the documentation of Greater Manchester's post-1945 churches a pressing matter.

Documentation

Architecture is a visual art, and its documentation has typically included photographs, architectural drawings, and, more recently, film. Visual representations, however, are always partial and reflect the bias of the documenter. The process of architectural documentation, and indeed its dissemination, has led to stylised architectural photographs which provide only a narrow view of buildings.[8] Despite recent trends amongst architectural historians to move away from textual narratives that privilege the built artefact, visual evidence all too often precludes wider context and evidence of use. In order to search out alternative representations, it was important to look beyond the sanctioned images of the architectural press, and to source photographs from, for example, church members who recorded the everyday activities of church life.

Photographic evidence of Greater Manchester's churches, for all its partiality, is substantial. A major source, maintained by Manchester Libraries, Information and Archives, is *Greater Manchester Lives*; a vast archive drawn from an eclectic range of sources which, collectively, documents aspects of Greater Manchester's social history. Even here though, we discovered black and white images of pristine newly

St Chad, Limeside (1965) by Paterson Macaulay & Owens.

minted buildings, predominantly taken by the city surveyors department. As such, these images frequently lacked the evidence of church and community life that we had encountered on our visits to the very same churches.

Those project architects responsible for overseeing and documenting the construction of the churches proved another rich source of material for our research. Records kept by the architectural firm of Paterson Macaulay & Owens, for example, gave an insight into the communities who built the now demolished St Chad, Limeside (1965). The photograph opposite brings to attention one group often overlooked in the architectural narrative—the local labourers, one of whom is seen here clambering over a skeletal roof structure without safety harness or hardhat.

As major institutions, church organisations were also a useful source of material. The Roman Catholic Diocese of Salford, for example, maintains extensive archives which includes an almost complete collection of the 'northern' edition of the Catholic Building Review and commemorative material relating to the history of its churches. Materials gathered by the clergy and congregants, however, are often kept at the churches themselves. Such documents were crucial in understanding local historical contexts and the life of church communities beyond Sunday worship, and revealed how such communities chose to document their buildings and the everyday activities that took place within them: after all, it is the users who make a building once construction is complete.

Increasing the type of sources has wider worth. The English system of heritage protection is skewed towards historic buildings and, more subjectively, those of architectural interest. In terms of Greater Manchester's post-1945 churches, it is buildings such as St Raphael, Stalybridge (1963) by Massey and Massey and St Jude, Wigan (1965) by L. A. G. Prichard & Son, deemed to be of artistic (therefore architectural) value, that are privileged. Yet such churches are less prevalent across the area surveyed. In order to not overlook the contribution of those buildings marginalised under present national listing criteria, a different approach to documentation is needed to capture the connection between the use of a building and its architectural qualities. The consultation of a wider array of source material, described above, partly achieves this through focussing on the way that different communities choose to document the history of churches.

Appreciation

The intention for Sacred Suburbs was to raise awareness of examples of post–1945 church design across Greater Manchester and to disseminate this through an exhibition and a publication. For the 2015 exhibition, we selected ten images to characterise the *Sacred Suburbs* project (see opposite). These comprised part of a wider exhibition called *ManModSoc*, which featured photographs of twentieth century Greater Manchester. Keen to reflect the documentation process, we struck a balance between traditional architectural photography, whilst giving due attention to the community aspects of church life. Consequently, we hinged the exhibition on the idea of contrasts.

Two images, of Church of the Ascension, Hulme (1970) by Robert Maguire and Keith Murray, and Coverdale Christian Church, Ardwick (1970) by Howard and Seddon, were chosen to demonstrate their contrasting scale with the housing estates in which they were located; these respectively being the Hulme Crescents and Coverdale Crescent (the latter disparagingly renamed 'Fort Ardwick' by its then residents). Both buildings have, because of regeneration, lost their original context and the sense of scale is now not apparent. Further contrasts were to be found in images of the church interiors. The elderly congregants of Wesley Methodist Church, Hulme (by J. C. G. Prestwich & Sons 1968) seemed incongruous in their modern surroundings. Meanwhile, everyday street scenes revealed how the modern church fitted into suburban contexts: the roof of St Hilda, Northenden (by Lanner Ltd 1970) seen rising above the traditional semi-detached houses, provides the backdrop to the sight of a young mother pushing a pram through the leafy suburb of Northenden.

When it came to a print publication, we chose to document at least one church from each of the ten Greater Manchester local authorities to show the varying expressions of post–1945 church building across the conurbation. In some cases, we were oversupplied: the large Wythenshawe estate to the south of Manchester is known to be replete with fine architectural examples but we limited ourselves to only one: George Pace's William Temple Memorial Church (1965) whose importance is not locally appreciated. Trying to represent a spread across the considered Christian groups also meant balancing the chosen examples. As noted above, the Roman Catholic Church and the Church of England examples were the most prevalent. However, there was much appeal in the simple form of Eccles Congregational Church, Eccles (1969) by T. D. Howcroft (see p.64). This was designed to replace an old church that was demolished to make way for the

Images from 'Sacred Suburbs', ManModSoc exhibition.

Eccles Congregational Church, Eccles (1969) by T. D. Howcroft.

South Lancashire Motorway. The floor plan allows for a multitude of concurrent uses, and is popular with local community groups.

*

Throughout the process of documenting, exhibiting, and publishing our research, we strove to highlight the community life of the post-1945 church by including views that are not always readily chosen in traditional visual accounts, such as those showing the buildings in their residential context. This emerged from a belief that documentation should capture the specificity of time, spatial context, and use. Even modernist buildings, often said to eschew historic context, are influenced by their surrounding environment and appropriated by their users once complete. Current methods of evaluation, which privilege the material aspects of the building, would do well to consider wider impact and use. Not all churches are of architectural importance, yet they are the buildings where people spend their daily lives at work, play, or worship. These are the churches that we may regularly walk past, which blend into the landscape; "it is this immersion which prevents us from seeing the everyday".[9]

---

1 Benefice of Manchester, The Good Shepherd and St Barnabas (Diocese of Manchester), Church Commissioners Pastoral Committee, Mission and Pastoral Measure, n.d., p.5.

2 *ManModSoc*: a photographic exhibition held at the offices of Stephen Hodder Associates, Manchester, 15 to 29 June 2015. Part of the AHRC's 'Connected Communities Festival'.

3 Angela Connelly and Matthew Steele, *Sacred Suburbs*, Manchester: The Modernist Society, 2015.

4 For example: Robert Proctor, *Building the Modern Church: Roman Catholic Church Architecture in Britain, 1955 to 1975*, Farnham: Ashgate, 2014.

5 David Voas and Alistair Crockett, 'Religion in Britain: Neither Believing nor Belonging', *Sociology* 39:1, 2005, pp.11–28.

6 Peter Brierley, 'Estimated Church Attendance, 1980–2015', British Religion in Numbers, brin.ac.uk/wp-content/uploads/2016/06/Estimated-Church-Attendance-1980-2015-Brierley.xlsx

7 Staff reporter. 2015. Bishop proposes halving number of parishes in Salford diocese, Catholic Herald, 23 November. Available at: catholicherald.co.uk/news/2015/11/23/salford-diocese-announces-plan-to-close-half-of-its-parishes/

8 Elizabeth McKellar, 'Representing the Georgian: Constructing Interiors in Early Twentieth Century Publications, 1890–1930', *Journal of Design History*, 20:4, 2007, pp.325–344.

9 Sarah Wigglesworth and Jeremy Till, 'The Everyday and Architecture', *The Everyday and Architecture*, edited by Sarah Wigglesworth and Jeremy Till, London: Architectural Design, 1998, (Architectural Design Profile, no.134) p.7.

From the series 'Orchard Park', Andy Lock, 2003.

ANDY LOCK, IN COLLABORATION WITH IAIN ANDERSON

The use of photography in recording the legacy of the modern movement in Britain's post-war landscapes

While there is currently a vogue for the sympathetic renovation and redevelopment of certain buildings dating from the decades of reconstruction immediately following World War II in Britain, many other buildings from the same era will instead be erased from the landscapes which they have helped to make distinctive. In some cases this might be the cue for popular resistance and debate, though more often than not, such demolition simply marks an uncermonious and quiescent end for buildings which have proven materially outmoded; burdensome to run and maintain, inappropriate to altered requirements. At such a terminal point in their biographies, perhaps the only professionals interested in photographing these economically moribund buildings are those tasked with recording the archaeology of the country's built heritage and artists, like myself.

As a photographer I was first drawn to post-war modern movement buildings as subjects for my work by the presence of their carcasses sitting, often forlornly, in varying states of neglect, amid provincial British landscapes, typically on the peripheries of the towns and cities in which I have lived and to which I have always been drawn when making photographs. In these settings, such buildings often seemed to represent the Ozymandian stumps of an entirely other historical trajectory.

In 2012, I began an informal, ongoing collaboration and dialogue with a colleague at Historic Environment Scotland (HES),[1] Iain Anderson, based on our mutual interest in the photographic recording and representation of the architectures of this period.[2] Over the past four years, this has led me to make photographs at a number of sites around Scotland which have also been subject to photographic survey by HES.

'Presbytery, St Bride's Church, East Kilbride', Andy Lock, 2014.

Here I outline the characteristics of the two quite differently motivated approaches to photographing modern movement buildings, represented by my own practice and the surveys carried out by HES. My focus is on images of one building, Castlemilk West Parish Church in Glasgow, in order to illustrate the ways in which the recording of decorative, architectonic and topographic information is simultaneously an engagement with a breadth of other ideas, preoccupations and narratives, which in turn, serve to enrich our understanding of a building's history or biography. This discussion has implications both for the diversity of photographic practices that might legitimately contribute to a 'heritage' architectural archive, and the potential for the photographic material in such collections to be read creatively and in ways unanticipated by the archive's formal remit.

Three distinct orders of 'modern' architecture have appeared repeatedly in my work: the educational, the domestic and the religious. Many of my photographs are preoccupied with the metaphysical possibilities as much as the physical properties of these buildings. It is not uncommon for my images to pursue some transcendent quality in representing such typically anonymous, domestic or institutional spaces as that seen on page 66, an image from the 2003 series, *Orchard Park*, made in a residential tower block on the eponymously named estate, located on the outskirts of Kingston upon Hull.

Post World War II modern movement churches also hold a fascination for me. In addition to constituting expressions of parochial community, they represent instances of buildings wherein we encounter a deliberate attempt to create in material, architectural terms, a vessel to hold something intangible and transcendent; a site designed to encompass experiences of an ineffable or sublime character. Somewhat perversely however, my images of these churches have tended to eschew a direct engagement with the architecture of the buildings itself and seem instead preoccupied with apparent trivialities. These are representations where intimations of an ecstatic reverie, often conveyed by nothing more tangible than a certain quality or fall of light, vie with the material evidence of buildings, which in contrast appear as little more than husks; their accumulations of furniture and the paraphernalia they contain, frequently tawdry or banal though undeniably poignant (as opposite, an image of St Bride's Church's presbytery, in East Kilbride).

HES for its part has a statutory responsibility for undertaking the detailed and systematic recording of a wide range of buildings in Scotland. Its photographic record-making typically occurs as part of a reactive survey process, often triggered by the imminent demolition or remodeling of the site in question. Notable examples of modern movement architecture form an increasingly significant constituent of this survey programme. Amongst such sites is Castlemilk West Parish Church in Glasgow, designed by Gratton & McLean Architects in 1957 and now listed, but threatened with demolition. The church has become a site of mutual interest for myself and HES. In 2013, the organisation documented the building in a series of fifty-three photographs, which range from the general to the specific.[3] Typically in an HES survey, the building is shown within its wider landscape context and in elevation; internally, key vistas and spaces are documented. Individual elements of built fabric and furniture, which together combine to build up the character of a space are recorded: windows, staircases and fireplaces, and finally the details of the building: lettering, ironmongery, any decorative or constructional detailing.

Above: 'Vestry, showing sloping window, Castlemilk West Parish Church', HES, 2013.
Below: 'Vestry with Church and Community mosaic, Castlemilk West', Andy Lock, 2013.

The vestry of the Castlemilk West church, a room of limited architectural consequence, was recorded in a single photograph within the HES survey (see opposite, above). As indicated by its caption, the image's primary function was not to record the detail of the interior of the room itself, but to record the room's distinctively shaped window, demonstrating where the mid-level rooms within the building sit in relation to the (exterior) distribution of windows around the base of the church. The image cannot, however, help but incidentally record the furnishing and décor of the vestry; the thin curtains which frame and partially obscure the window, the plastic chair and the items of highly polished institutional furniture which populate the room; the mosaic and clock above an electric fire, just protruding into shot. Despite ostensibly engaging with the building's architectural features, the image also, albeit inadvertently, reveals the multitude of ways in which the church's users and inhabitants have played a cumulative role in shaping the building's ultimate character and biography; not least in maintaining a scrupulously tended interior at odds with the church's exterior condition.

My own approach to photographing at Castlemilk West was at once less systematic, more selective and more partial in its selection and treatment of subjects, than the work of HES. Of the images I made during a number of brief visits to the church, perhaps the most compelling (opposite, below) also concerns the church's vestry and occupies itself with the small mosaic and the electric fire that we see peripherally in the HES image of the same room. The mosaic, entitled 'Church and Community' was presented to Castlemilk's congregation in 1966 by C. Guy, an elder of the church. It depicts the church and its erstwhile arch and spire (later removed for safety reasons). The church's entrance is shown framed by trees, and ranged behind the church we see what appear to be tenements and blocks of flats, rising in ranks. The mosaic itself—like so many photographs of architecture, and in contrast to my own and HES' images—shows the building as new, perfected. It conveys an aspirant, utopian vision of the church at the forefront and in the midst of its community.

In common with the image of the St Bride's church presbytery, my photograph of the Castlemilk fire and mosaic is an unashamedly poignant image, whose contents highlight a theme that suffuses an encounter with the site. The mosaic and the architecture of the building it represents were both, when new, symbolic of the church's place at the forefront of Castlemilk's future, in terms of design, lifestyle and the pastoral care of the new city suburb. While the mosaic continues to attest to this aspiration, the current state of its referent and its relationship to its environs now serve to suggest the church's increasing marginalisation in the face of subsequent developments in all of these spheres. If the mosaic presents the church as the literal and metaphorical centrepiece of a carefully composed, new civic and pastoral vision at Castlemilk, then a contemporary photographic account of the site, particularly one which emphasises topographic views of the church and its immediate surroundings, allows us to capture something of the idealism of that particular historical moment, in the context of subsequent historical developments and vicissitudes.

Although HES has documented the exterior of the church, these images tend to focus on the fabric of the building itself, with its environs playing a literally peripheral role in the photographs (see opposite, above). By comparison, in terms of their framing, my own images of the church's exterior depict the building as more determinedly a part of its surroundings (turning back to look at both from a distance, rather than treating the church as a centrepiece and its surroundings as a mere backdrop). The photograph opposite, below, reveals something of the church's present discontinuity from its surroundings. The representation makes apparent the recent renovation of adjacent tenements and (in the foreground of the image) the extensive site clearance of many others; actions which have left the degraded corpus of the church as a conspicuously ruinous component in the city's landscape. The building remains extant, but as the image implies, it is an increasingly manifest anachronism in relation to its surroundings. What my image of the mosaic and fire intimates about an outmoded, idealist vision through a synecdoche, the topographic images of the church clarify through juxtaposition. While the Castlemilk West church still clearly retains its role as a locus for community activity, the building's all too apparent material marginalisation within the landscape seems emblematic of a gradual forgetting of its idealistic naissance; a naissance encapsulated by the 'Church and Community' mosaic.

At the time of writing, in summer 2016, the Church of Scotland has Castlemilk West Parish Church listed as for sale and development. The photograph on the cover of the sale brochure shows the church

Above: 'View from North West, Castlemilk West Parish Church'. HES, 2013.
Below: 'Castlemilk West Parish Church'. Andy Lock, 2013.
Left: *Church of Scotland sales brochure, 2016.*

framed by a grove of trees, tenements rising in the background behind it. Given the function of the brochure, it is difficult not to regard this latest and perhaps final, formal image of the building as a deeply ironic photographic echo of the church's depiction in the 1966 'Church and Community' mosaic.

The imminent displacement of the Castlemilk church's congregation, implicit in a 'development' such as the one proposed for the church's site, highlights a further theme shared by my own practice and the work of the HES photographic survey. I noted earlier that the survey's photographic record-making is often triggered by the prospect of imminent demolition or the remodeling of a site. My own photographic work for its part is repeatedly drawn, albeit intuitively rather than systematically, to subjects which are similarly characterised either by displacement or the imminent prospect of displacement. In addition to Castlemilk West itself, for example, the deserted rooms in the images that comprise the *Orchard Park* series (see p.66) were the product of the displacement of inhabitants from many dozens of apartments. I wouldn't want to reduce the significance of buildings like Castlemilk West to the status of mere cyphers in my work through which I am able to explore themes such as 'displacement', but the recurrence in my practice of examples of such architecture is I believe, due at least in part to a unique complex of material and design flaws, demographic trends and social and economic changes, which have combined to create no shortage of post-war modern movement buildings of so precarious a status as to offer rich opportunities to explore such themes. My work on the Castlemilk West church thus represents an instance of an approach to photographing buildings which is strongly inflected by personal preoccupations beyond architecture itself, but which nonetheless finds not only a compelling resonance with contemporary social and economic themes, but also a meeting point with the concerns of a statutory process of recording architecture 'at risk'.

We can see how my own images of the Castlemilk West church, HES' survey photographs, and the Church of Scotland's sales brochure all contribute to the sum of the photographic representations of the building. In addition to these representations we might expect to find photographs made for the architectural press when the church was newly constructed. However, there is an apparent gap in the record in the case of Castlemilk West. More generally, where such architectural photographs of newly built modern movement buildings dating from the 1950s and 1960s have found their way into an archive, such as that of the Royal Institute of British Architects (RIBA) or HES, they have—through their role in subsequent publications—done much to shape our interpretation not just of the fabric, but of the cultural meaning of the modern architecture from this era.[4] The rhetoric of these photographs; their often austere, portentously futuristic, monochrome visions, also provides a powerful context for our reading of subsequent images like my own or those of HES. It is hard not to read these representations from the present in the light of the utopian visions of the recent past.

In examining how, as in the case of Castlemilk West church, a range of photographic images resulting from different practices and different preoccupations contribute to the construction of the record of a building, the need to challenge the plausibility of the notion of either a comprehensive or definitive photographic record becomes evident. The photographs discussed above, with their different intentions, intended audiences and rhetoric, serve to illustrate the diversity of practices and sources which can, over time, contribute to the photographic record of a modern movement building. As Beatriz Colomina, writing in 1996, in *Privacy and Publicity: Modern Architecture as Mass Media*, noted, a record largely constituted by images will in many cases outlive a modern movement building itself and play a decisive role in shaping its legacy. In examining the *legacy* of such a building, the photographic archive—conceived in its broadest sense—arguably represents as important a terrain to explore as a site in the landscape, such as the one currently occupied by Castlemilk West Parish Church.[5]

---

1 The Royal Commission on the Ancient and Historical Monuments of Scotland (RCAHMS) merged with Historic Scotland in 2015 to form HES.

2 This dialogue and previous papers co-written with Iain Anderson inform this writing.

3 A full selection of survey images are available at canmore.org.uk

4 See for example Robert Elwall, *Building a Better Tomorrow: Architecture in Britain in the 1950s*, Wiley, 2000.

5 In *Privacy and Publicity: Modern Architecture as Mass Media* (MIT Press, 1996), Beatriz Colomina proposes that Modern Architecture became modern as a consequence of its engagement with the mass media and that its significant sites were to be found not on individual building plots, but on the pages of mass print media (pp.14–15). The archive represents a significant site for Colomina too, and was implicated in the redrawing of boundaries between public and private, which characterised the new spatial dispensation she describes (p.9).

EDDY RHEAD

From Here to Modernity— Manchester Modernist Society

There is a glaring contradiction at the heart of the Manchester Modernist Society that, as one of its founders, I am acutely aware of. The word Modernist in the group's name seems at odds with much of the subject matter that we take an interest in precisely because we tend to focus on the past. Be it in architecture, design, art or social history, we openly admit to a certain nostalgia for the immediate post-war period, an era when modernism thrived and seemed certain to change the world forever.

We have sometimes received criticism that we can't consider ourselves true Modernists because of our obsession with the past, but that accusation makes the assumption that there is some intellectual and academic rigour in what we do. Whilst we surround ourselves with academics and through them make some attempt to add new and important research to various disciplines, we always try to make what we do fun, creative and entertaining, treading a fine line between unashamed populism and intellectual worthiness.

When the Society was formed in 2009 there was little or no aspiration to become anything formal or organised. Jack Hale and Maureen Ward, two friends who shared a common interest in the city of Manchester and modernist architecture and design, were somewhat frustrated that whilst Manchester's Victorian architectural heritage was well known and celebrated, its twentieth century buildings were at best overlooked and at worst maligned. The early activities of the Manchester Modernist Society were devised primarily as a creative art project. There was never any desire to be a conservation or campaign-

Left: 'Toastrack' publication, 2013.

ing group, and engaging creatives has always been at the core of what we do.

Though they had experience in managing arts projects, Jack and Maureen were, by their own admission, keen amateurs when it came to Manchester's architectural history. With fortuitous timing I was looking for a channel for my energies around the time the Society was forming. I had been involved with the Twentieth Century Society for several years, helping to form the North West Group and organising events in the north west. I had, however, grown frustrated with what I saw as a too London-centric approach and was finding conservation campaigning a little too negative and soul destroying. The nascent Manchester Modernist Society had the energy and positivity I was looking for, and they were more than happy to add my knowledge of Manchester's twentieth century architecture into the mix.

Early events were very informal but met with enthusiasm by the public. The first was an urban picnic where people were invited via social media to come and meet like-minded individuals. Such was the response that a small gathering turned into a respectable sized group. It soon became clear that there was an appetite for what the Manchester Modernist Society was aiming to do, and this is when we started to formalise the group into something more than idle fancy.

There were several legal matters that had to be arranged around setting up a not for profit group, but a more important matter was deciding on core principles. Luckily we were pretty clear on what we wanted to achieve with the Society and how we wanted to do it. We were never motivated by making money and wanted any events that we organised to be approachable as well as inclusive. Channelling a certain Reithian ideal we wanted to promote Manchester's twentieth century architectural heritage, but sought to do so in a fun and accessible way. We did not want our walks to be, or try to compete with, Blue Badge guides, and with our events we would always try to find subject matter that hadn't been covered before, or to provide a new angle.

An early example of this was when we discovered a film made about the construction of The Mancunian Way motorway. It was a relatively technical film which, if truth be told, was quite dull in parts, but we found a venue to show it and the event sold out. Feedback from the audience was positive and it was then that we realised that there were enough people interested to hold events on a regular basis and create a membership system for the group. It was here that we hit a small problem because the hastily thought up name of

Eddy Rhead leading a city centre walk in Manchester.

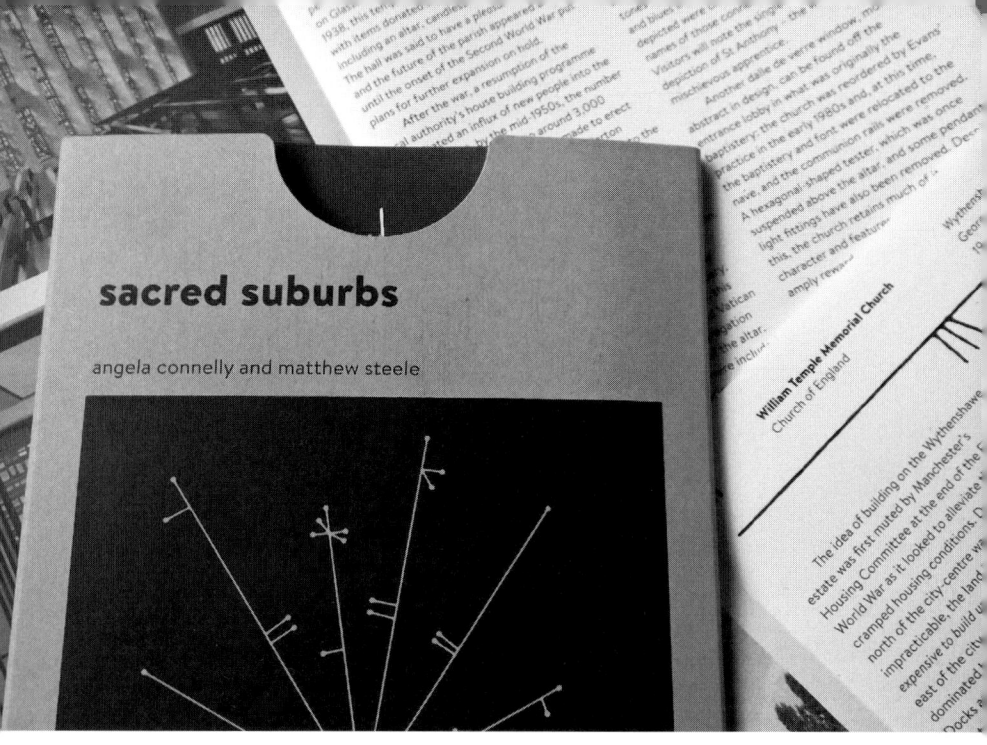

'Sacred Suburbs' publication, 2015.

the Manchester Modernist Society cheekily implied that we were a formal society whose wider membership could have voting rights and influence the direction of the group. This was never the intention; we had a clear idea of what we wanted, and thought a traditional membership would undermine that clarity of vision. Our membership is 'honorary' and members essentially support the society financially by joining so that we can continue doing what we do.

Another founding principle was the desire to constantly produce something creative. We felt that if we were a group centred on campaigning and conservation this would lead to negativity, but if we were a creative collective, positivity would prevail and this would keep us and our members motivated. While we are happy to lend support to campaigns that we care about and are relevant to our interests we have little desire to enter into battles with planning authorities, councils or property developers.

Anything we produce has to be of the highest quality and good design is central to any of our outputs. We have always been very lucky that creative people support what we do and offer their services, often for free. The Society could not survive without this goodwill but we are sure that if, as a group, you show integrity in what you do, others will recognise this and offer their services and time to help. We have developed strong links with various departments within the local universities, and this offers a rich vein of both academics and students who we can call on for both intellectual and artistic support in various projects. These collaborations have produced a variety of different projects in which we hope we have produced not only stimulating events but also a legacy that people interested in twentieth century design and architecture will draw on.

Over the past six years we have delivered many projects including installing a sound installation in a telephone box and designating the UMIST campus a conservation area. Two of our most successful projects have been *Toastrack* and *Sacred Suburbs*. *Toastrack* involved a year-long residency at the Hollings Campus, a Grade II listed building, that was being vacated by the Manchester Metropolitan University. Over the course of an academic year we immersed ourselves in the history of the building, running a regular blog, showing found items, archive material, ephemera and historical research, which culminated in a publication by Matthew Steele on the history of the building. We also threw a party, where we celebrated the building, which the original architect Derek Hill was able to attend. Students managed the party and also collaborated by designing a Toastrack Ale, beermats and a 'goody-bag'.

Mathew Steele is one of many regular collaborators and, along with Angela Connelly, was also responsible for the *Sacred Suburbs* project which looked at post-war churches in the Greater Manchester area. This culminated in an event with a seminar with various speakers and an afternoon bus trip to visit some of the churches identified in the research. There was a publication which brought together Matthew and Angela's research in an accessible and interesting printed format. Although much of the Modernist Society's activity is voluntary we do occasionally receive project funding to help us with our work. *Sacred Suburbs* was part of a Heritage Lottery Funded volunteer engagement project, though much goodwill was called upon in devising and delivering the project and designing the publication.

Publications are something the Manchester Modernist Society has always been interested in and are something we aim to expand. Not long after we started it became apparent that there were a significant number of people interested in what we were doing, and we had built an alliance of talented people who had the potential to write for us. It was from there that our magazine *The Modernist* was born. We started the magazine at a time when the death of print was being predicted so there was a great deal of uncertainty and nervousness. But five years later we are still producing a quarterly magazine with respectable sales both online and in outlets such as Tate Modern, Foyles and Waterstones. As with the Society, the magazine relies on a great deal of generosity in time and effort, but contributions are always forthcoming, with our aim being to strike a balance between the academic and populist. We take great pride in *The Modernist*'s high quality design, despite a very limited budget. We also hope to add other types of publications to our outputs, covering a variety of subject matter and formats—from pamphlets through to high quality books.

The Modernist magazine is read throughout the world and the articles reflect this international audience. The Manchester Modernist Society has also broken its own initial geographic boundaries and associated Modernist Societies have been set up in Sheffield and Liverpool, hopefully with other cities to follow. Post-war architecture and design is slowly but surely finding a wider and enthusiastic audience and we like to think we have helped build that audience. We are happy to foster, incubate and help grow this appreciation. As long as there is enthusiasm from the wider world for what we do, there will be enthusiasm from us to continue.

An archive of our projects can be found at modernist-society.org/projects

'The Modernist' magazine, issue 15 'Entertainment'.

SALLY STONE

Gate 81

Preston Bus Station is an extraordinary building. It was constructed in the same year as the first moon landing, 1969, and exhibits that same sense of confidence and optimism. It is an incredibly long and elegant structure and the architectural language of the building can be described as brutal, in that it is constructed from raw concrete. The building contains a series of car parks situated on extended floor plates with upturned curving parapets which appear to float over the double-height space of the public concourse. The interior still contains the original rubber flooring, timber benches and white-tiled walls. Building Design Partnership (BDP) architects designed the building and the concept was to emulate an airport; even the different bus stops were referred to as gates.

In late 2012, the City Council proposed its demolition and replacement with a surface car park. They considered that the prohibitively high conservation costs combined with the prime location of the site meant that the destruction of the building could act as a prime factor in the regeneration of a quite depressed city.

This provocative act galvanised various groups that were already campaigning to save the building and proved to be the impetus for a number of different types of projects. Gate 81, one of foremost of these groups, was a collaboration between an academic, an architect and an arts organisation. They curated a collection of events based in and around the bus station with the intention of raising the profile of the building. There had been a considerable amount of negativity surrounding the future of the bus station, and Gate 81 intended to bring some optimism to the situation. The aims of the group were to be deliberately non-antagonistic; that is, provocative but not confrontational. It was not about demands, demonstration and protest, rather Gate 81 wanted to celebrate and appreciate the building; indeed,

Left: *View from the underpass looking towards the floating parapets of the car park. The curving concrete upstands were cast using an innovative system of fibreglass moulds; this was a significant factor in the listing of the structure.*

explicit within the manifesto was the intention to "…enjoy the building while we still can", and with reference to the airport-style agenda of the original architects: "Preston Bus Station has 80 Gates, we'd like to keep it this way".

The campaign was successful, and the Bus Station was granted a Grade II Listing. This means that any redevelopment of the city has to consider the presence of a huge modernist masterpiece at the heart of any proposal. In 2014 the collection of various pressure groups were presented with the government sponsored Heritage Alliance award. They specifically cited the Save the Preston Bus Station campaign as a "phenomenal example of people power" and a fine example of how it is possible to save a piece of heritage through public pressure.

The ground floor interior: the building still contains the original timber barriers, white ceramic wall tiles and rubber floor. Note the clocks which show the time in both digital and analogue.

Preparations for the Gate 81 workshop or Hac-Lab: this public event was situated in the north-end of the building. The canvas screen allowed for a certain amount of acoustic and visual control.

The Gate 81 Hac-Lab was a collection of different activities held on the ground floor of the building on a cold and rainy day in May. The cultural importance of the bus station was discussed and debated; even representatives of the city council joined in.

Artist Chris Jones grew up in the city and vividly remembers as a child riding in the passenger seat of his parent's car as they glided up the curving ramps to the car park. He created an installation based upon the memory of this experience in one of the unused ground floor shop units.

BDP Architects sponsored a very serious design charrette, which was attended by local and national architects and designers. The focus was on the creation of an urban plan that would reconnect the bus station with the city.

Antwerp Interrupted: The problem of the massive modernist structure situated within the heart of a traditional city was the subject of a design workshop at the University of Antwerp

The final event was a joyous procession though the streets of Preston. The participants carried aloft an enormous fragmented model of the building; the journey concluded in the sunshine of the Bus Station forecourt.

Film Still, Rooms With a View, 2008.

VERITY-JANE KEEFE

The Mobile Museum

Outer London Prologue

Getting the train into Barking from Walthamstow Queens Road in 2006. Looking into the backyards of industry, housing estates and shops the train line sliced through the northern edges of inner London via E17 into the depths of Outer London proper. The city would run out, open out and suburbia would begin within two stops.

I took this train three or four times a week for a year or so whilst working on a project for the architecture practice I worked for. A huge 1960s landscape format block of flats dominated the skyline and announced the arrival into Barking station. The Lintons was overclad in an optimistic blue and red geometric pattern which seemed appropriate in the 1990s. This landscape became temporarily so familiar, imagining what played out within the blocks, the ambient soundscapes you'd hear from the platform, the matchbox shaped block at odds with the other nearby towers. This block represented the beginning of an ongoing, deep, often tumultuous and passionate love affair with Outer London, and in particular Barking and Dagenham's position within it.

The Lintons was earmarked for demolition and was pulled down following a long decanting process in 2007. I remember feeling genuine sadness when I heard it was to be demolished, followed by confusion and the desire to unpick what this sadness meant to me as an artist. How a building that had temporarily become iconic within my everyday would disappear. A lot has happened since then to get from Barking Town Square, via The Lintons to The Mobile Museum.

Research Narrative / The Mobile Museum

The Mobile Museum is an ex local authority mobile library 2001 Ford Iveco. It has had a variety of creative past lives: as a mobile library in rural Wales, as a temporary art commission in East London looking

The Mobile Museum, icons of place, 2015.

at nature in the city, as a reggae and dub recording studio / outdoor living room on a farm in Glastonbury, to The Mobile Museum. It has been loved, neglected, reborn and loved again. The initial ambition and agenda was to transform the interior of the vehicle into an itinerant museum that tours the borough's twelve remaining purpose built council estates, collecting, making, gathering and responding along the way, and constructing a new natural history collection based on the evolution of the council house. Speculative, playful, rigorous and grounded in natural history modes of display and taxonomies, inside The Mobile Museum, the development of council housing is used as a timeline to order the collection and tour the borough, working with a mixture of residents, council staff members and interested people from further afield.

The Mobile Museum grew out of a desire to celebrate the glorious everyday rhythms of Barking and Dagenham—as a looking glass to reflect wider Outer London—via its housing estates and the people

that live in them. What is and can the artist's role and potential(s) within regeneration contexts be? Can we, as artists (and people) do more than provide consultation fodder or tick boxes within a wider development framework? Can we interrogate and question 'value'? What was valued from a commissioner's perspective but more importantly from a resident, shopkeeper or council staff member's perspective? The Mobile Museum as an initial idea, sought to test and interrogate buzzwords that had become synonymous with work delivered in the public realm: regeneration, participation, consultation, collaboration, community, engagement, resilience, authorship and legacy, all buzzwords that get chucked all over the place, on hoardings, in funding applications, in artist briefs and in client's desires.

In September 2012 the local authority match funding for The Mobile Museum was cut in the first wave of public sector cuts. This represented a significant sea change in my practice. Politics with a capital p and politics dominated. It represented the need for me to wear many hats and be fundraiser, pitcher, strategist, personal cheerleader and

Interior, The Mobile Museum, February 2016.

policy negotiator. To maintain relationships. To maintain my own interest in the area, and housing estates, a couple of which were demolished during the process.

By September 2014 I had successfully raised the deficit via a Kickstarter campaign. 346 people donated, the majority of them unknown to me from the fields of art, architecture, planning, urban studies, geography, museums and collections, from grass roots campaigners, fans of modernism and more. Something so locally positioned seemed to resonate with an international audience. People were drawn to the politics of funding cuts, the challenges of producing work in the current climate without compromise, of the value that existed in an often maligned area, a borough tarred with all manner of assumptions and stereotypes. The re-presenting of these places via the collection and through documentation of the process created a new living archive, which it seemed, a lot of people were interested in. The work felt more important, more public. The process of crowd funding helped construct support and an audience before the work was made, it addressed the public sector crisis and confirmed the importance of The Mobile Museum's role in connecting disparate strands of local authority provision (libraries, culture, housing, education) by driving into the heart of the communities, lurking, looking and responding.

The Becontree Estate is known to be an absolute marvel, a planning trailblazer with it's 81 different 'types' of dwellings, the utopian optimism of wave after wave of east enders moving to Dagenham after the Addison Act (1919) to find an inside toilet and a generous garden, complete with ready made community spirit, rules and regulations. But what about other estates like Marks Gate and Thames View, the north and south bookends of the borough, both absolutely dripping in 1950s civic pride, both feeling very different to each other and Becontree in turn. How can these feelings, the differences and similarities be captured? How can The Mobile Museum / Collection / Artwork (delete as appropriate) become a useful tool to local authority officers, developers and planners, to inform future planning policy and regeneration decisions? The Museum attempts to present a realistic and vivid portrait via residents and objects of what it is actually like to live in these places: on the 17th floor of (now demolished) Ingrave House, or the mid-rise blocks of Keir Hardie Way. Ingrave House was once an engineering example of best practice, and ended its life as the leaky, tired looking home to 96 flats. The experience of living there within the shadows of the 1960s planners' ambitions is intricately different to that in the mid-rise blocks of Keir Hardie Way, flanked in flora and fauna and inter-war curved brick porches. The Mobile Museum's activities have responded to these local contexts at every stage: *Make Your Own Protest Banner* at Keir Hardie Way, at Marks Gate, site casting and mark making, at Thames View a *Walk to View the Thames*, an archaeological dig for the Gascoigne, currently mid way through demolition, *Make Your Own Model Village* for Ibscott Close, built on the site of the former Dagenham Village and much more.

A project that was supposed to last twelve weeks is now in its fourth year. One year applying for, developing and securing the funding, one year picking up the pieces after losing some of the funding and two years of delivery. It still feels like the beginning, like it's just begun. The landscape has changed so much since those early train journeys in awe of The Lintons and is still changing. The Mobile Museum is able to respond to these changes live, to record them and archive them. A new chapter of social history is being documented and accessioned, through The Mobile Museum, to the borough archives. The collection tells the story of these once thirteen, now eleven emblems of planning, and through these buildings, of utopian visions, their occupants, the borough and London as a whole.

There is something addictive in the ordinariness, peculiarity and familiarity of Outer London, particularly my relationship with Barking and Dagenham. There is the constant hankering for improvement and progress from both residents and local authorities. There is culture-led regeneration waving the flag for this progress often in tandem with the mechanical long reach arm of demolition and the slow decline of local, large scale industry. At the same time, there is a rapid influx of new residents all wanting, needing, somewhere to live and work.

It's very complex. I don't think there are any firm conclusions, just commas and permutations. I keep hinting at my exit strategy from working within the borough but with such wild large scale planning schemes on the table, I'm not sure how I could retreat. The lure of Barking Riverside—described on the website as "A brand new neighbourhood… being created alongside two km of Thames river frontage at Barking Riverside, one of the most ambitious and important new developments in the UK… on the former power station site"—and its 10,800 new homes. Looking over the river to Thamesmead, a remnant of earlier planning now being comprehensively redeveloped, thinking about how that dialogue will work. Once Thamesmead and Riverside are fully developed, there will be a joint conurbation rivaling the size of Derby. A whole new pair of towns.

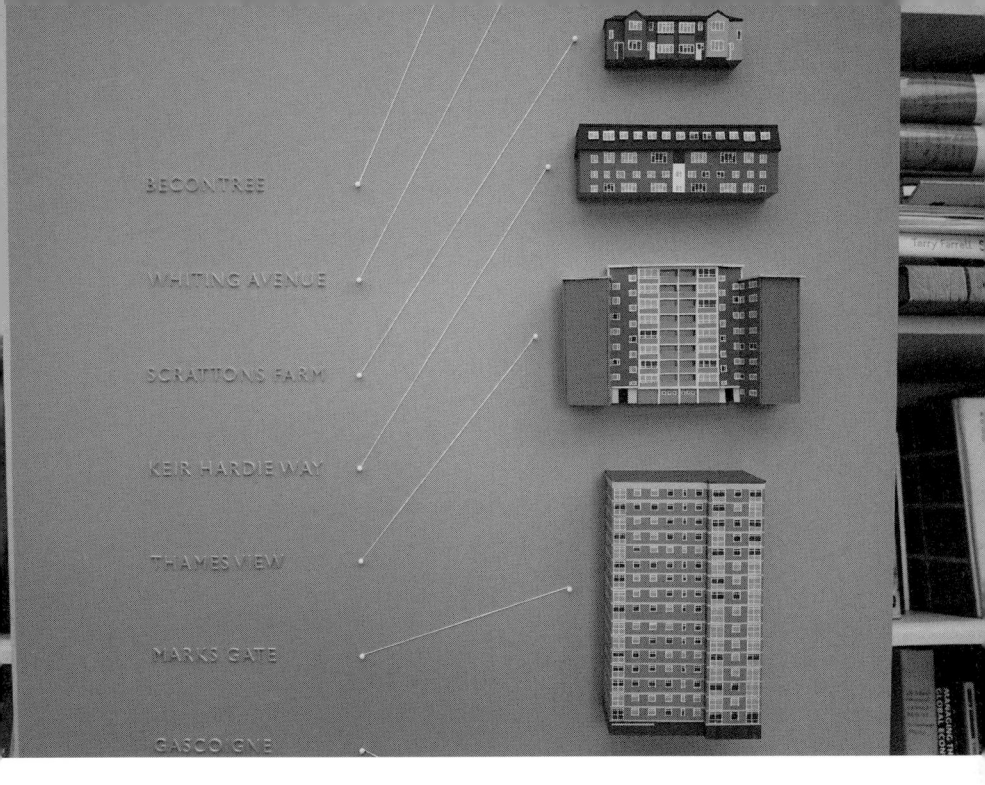

Council estate building typology evolution model, inside The Mobile Museum.

 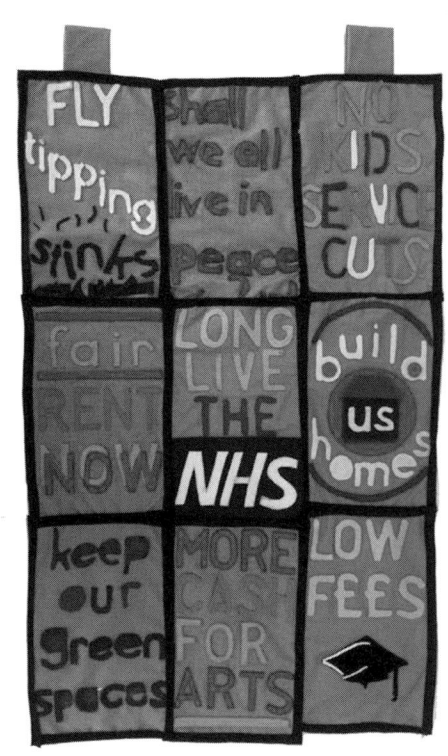

Left: Marks Gate Estate Soil Sample, The Mobile Museum Collection, 2015.

Right: Keir Hardie Way Estate Protest Banner, made with residents to document everyday protests, The Mobile Museum Collection, 2015.

Decanting Process Epilogue (Legacy)

I have taken my LGV driving test, am now eligible to drive a bus or similar should all else fail, have an enviable Honesty Lending Library (crowd sourced from my Kickstarter backers and a wider academic and not so academic network), oak parquet flooring, and a huge scar on my leg from an accident the day before the launch. The Mobile Museum Trust, a supporting cast of invited boffins and intellects that represent the various threads of the project, is established to ensure I am making the right decisions, to act as a sounding board and to accompany me whilst I go in the ring head to head with what the legacy of the project can be and find out what's possible. Things are built, emptied, demolished, people moved around. The same with The Mobile Museum. It's been built, existed and will be emptied of the collection at some point soon. Recording the social histories of residents alongside the stories of the staff that worked in these estates, from the housing officer to the concierge to the decanting officer, reveals how each has their own role within the regeneration process. I'm just lucky enough to have been able to record these as part of a much larger story, playing my own role within the process.

IAN WAITES

'Spontaneous Estate Evolution' Research/Practice interventions on a 1960s council estate

What do we do with the post-World War Two council estate? With those environments of the modernist era that are routinely and stereotypically viewed as grim, outdated, rundown and almost worthless? Even a *Guardian* article seems to perpetuate the same old tired tropes:

> "The grey, pebble dashed frontages of 1950s council houses are not improved by rain... the mistakes of the post-war planners of public housing have long been derided—from the materials they used (too much concrete) to the scale they built on (too monolithic) and the places where they chose to build (too far from the middle of town)."[1]

In 1964, when I was three years old, my family moved to a brand new house on a brand new council estate in a town called Gainsborough, Lincolnshire. The Middlefield Lane estate was a typical product of post-war local and central government policy intended to provide new, modern, rented housing for families of all kinds, and it was full of those 'mistakes' that post-war planners and architects apparently made. Our house had a pebble-dashed frontage, the centrepiece of the estate was a fairly monolithic, modernist complex of shops, 'link-maisonettes', underpasses and flats. The estate was built on the edge of the town, looking out onto open countryside, and it was planned as an open-plan pedestrianised environment where the car was restricted to only two access roads in favour of short terraces of houses that were grouped around communal green areas and public footpaths.

Left: *Back to the Future 1965–2015–2016 on Aisby Walk, August 2015.*

Aerial view of the estate, 1972.

For the past four years or so, I've been working on what I call a 'deep history' of this estate—an interpretive, sometimes even poetic evaluation of its history and of its 'meaning'. Specifically, I explore the way the estate was designed and planned in relation to the more subjective considerations of memory and belonging. I pore over archive photographs like this aerial view of the estate, doing what Freud described as memory work, attempting to situate myself back in the estate as it was in the 1960s and 70s, trying to remember what it *felt like* to live there.

The phrase 'Spontaneous Estate Evolution' comes from Alison Ravetz's book *Council Housing and Culture: The History of a Social Experiment* (2001). The book is generally well disposed towards the idea of the council estate, but it still manages to be sniffy about post-war council estates, which, according to Ravetz, were the product of: "a vision forged by one section of society for application to another… It asked nothing more of tenants than to live in houses

and to participate in estate life in ways approved by middle-class reformers... a situation that precluded any *spontaneous estate evolution* [my italics]."²

Regardless of how this expresses the tired but still very common notion that the working classes somehow became bland surburbanites after they were rehoused on these estates, brainwashed by middle-class planners and architects who denied them the chance to make these estates work for themselves in a true, 'authentic' working class manner, the idea of a 'spontaneous estate evolution' is an interesting one, and one which I kept in mind when I began to do some collaborative research/practice work on the Middlefield Lane estate with two artists, Kate Genever and Steve Pool (aka The Poly-Technic), last summer.³

Kate and Steve caught wind of my research a couple of years ago, and they got in touch to see what we could do together. I like working with Kate and Steve because their credo is simple and direct: "With people, in places—doing things". So, in August 2015, I found myself involved in creating what might be called (in contemporary art-curatorial speak) 'transformative interventions', or 'happenings'—spontaneous estate evolutions even—as part of an ongoing project we called *Back to the Future 1965–2015–2016*. For three days, we set up a very basic, mock 1960s living room out on the estate to get the children who live there to come and hang out, to play with a 1960s dolls house and some 60s games—Buckaroo, Frustration and so on—and to get them to talk about their everyday lives on the estate (see p.102). We set up shop by a tree that had a tyre swing, and we soon got a number of children ranging in age from 3 to 11 coming along to see what was happening. Everyone was very open and receptive to what we were doing—parents and carers would call by soon after to ask what we were doing and why, and most of the children stayed with us all day. Some older boys on BMXs and skateboards came to see what we were doing but they drifted off quite quickly once they'd decided that it was rubbish.

Over those three days, we interviewed some of the children about where they played on the estate, what they did, and what they felt about where they lived. I did a tour of the estate to show them where I played when I was their age back in the 60s, and two of the children took us on a tour of 'their' estate, to the places that were significant to them. We filmed and photographed these tours as we went along, with an aim to produce a finished, edited, film of the event—and I soon came to realise that little had changed in the forty years or so since I was a kid there. It was a fine, sunny week during the summer holidays and *everyone* was playing out. The children showed us the walls they played football against, the cut-throughs between the blocks of houses where they cycled, and the dens they made on a piece of wasteland near the estate. These children played blocko and tig and kerby.

When we talked to them, they told us how time slowed down when they were bored and didn't know what to do, and of how it sped up and went far too quickly when they were into a particular game. We also played around with time itself when Steve enlarged an old 1967 photo of me and my friends and mounted it onto a board. He cut out a hole where my head was so that anyone could poke their face through and 'become' me, and to travel back in time, back to 1967. At one time, I took the board over to my house to send myself back in time and space, but there was a fence around my old front lawn containing a slightly lairy dog, and so we looked for the nearest equivalent, an empty house just a few doors down and took this photo of me (opposite), suspended in time between 1967 and 2015.

Time Travel on Dunstall Walk, August 2015.

Projection, October 2015.

The second phase of the project took place in early October when we went back to the estate to show the residents the films and photos we'd made in August—and we did this as a large scale projection—projected onto the estate itself. Again we attracted quite a crowd of children and adults—who took lots of photos of the projections, and of their children as they leapt about in front of the larger than life images of themselves enjoying those lost summer days. It was quite spectacular, and often quite beautiful, as I hope this photograph (opposite) demonstrates.

The next phase of the project, which I've named 'A New House just like the Old House, only New!' will involve occupying a house on the estate to recreate a living room based on what I remember of mine back in 1966. The space will be used for a public exhibition on the history of the estate, and to put on a display of artefacts collected from the residents, and which they think best represents their life on the estate.

So *why* am I doing this? What do I want to achieve? One way of answering this can be expressed in a statement that I've had to use in a funding bid for this project:

> "The project will connect people with their past and reconceptualise Middlefield Lane as a mutable place not always in decline… it will develop skills, connections and aspirations to help the community build for a better future; and champion council estates in a period lacking good, affordable, rented housing."

But while the general necessity of at least *attempting* to do something in respect of celebrating and championing 1960s council estates is indisputable, I worry about the imperatives here, and about the way they are expressed. Elsewhere, buzzwords like 'agency' and 'resilience' are often used in respect of 'changing communities'. Such terms are, at best, blandly technocratic. Worse, they are essentially meaningless, especially within a community like that at Middlefield which is made up of people with an array of often quite specific and individual needs, likes, cares and so on, and which can be very different to the ones that maybe we think they should have. As such, and as a former resident of the estate myself, I feel that I have to be constantly alert to the ambiguities and drawbacks of the project I'm describing here, and of its aims. Fifty or more years on from when these estates were first being conceived, are we still in danger of asking "nothing more of tenants than to… participate in estate life in ways approved by middle-class reformers"—situations that preclude any chance of a *spontaneous estate evolution*?

Is it therefore right to conceptualise the estate as a 'mutable' place, where the residents are busy trying to manage their lives in an already pluralistic, fragmented and unstable world? If the aims of a project like this are about connecting residents with the past, "developing skills, connections and aspirations to help the community build for a better future", then we should accept that this might not happen in the ways that we 'middle-class reformers' might want it to (and certainly not in accordance with the demands of remote academic research funding bodies). Either way, this suggests that we need to think more carefully about participation and difference, and about new ways of formulating creative community projects. And maybe we need to embrace the fact that a project like this might well produce unpredictable and unmeasurable results. We can't make the residents here have 'agency'. We can't chivvy them along into pulling together and in becoming resilient, however gently or creatively we might try to do it. Furthermore, and despite our attempts to reconfigure modernist architecture as part of a heritage agenda today, we certainly cannot expect residents to demand a reappraisal of where they live because we think of these estates as "great examples of the *architecture* of the welfare state".[4]

Any 'resilience' on an estate like Middlefield has to come from within. If that has no cause to happen then I'm happily reminded of what a colleague of mine once said about community arts in general: that maybe it's enough to do things that merely make a nice change, rather than them having to make a change. Out of all this, the academic in me has nevertheless been dipping into Guattari's *Three Ecologies*—and the one thing I've taken from this is the idea of creating "a new aesthetic, a new gentleness" as a starting point in getting "social and political practices back on their feet".[5] We are all living in an increasingly harsh, neo-liberal world (which has turned modernism into just another consumerist fetish, and which produces impersonal and slightly hubristic jargon like 'resilience' and 'agency') and so I'd like my work to hang onto that 'new gentleness', however idealistic that might be.

In order to help residents realise a connection between their everyday lives and the place where they live, the *Back to the Future* project aims to quietly and tacitly 'slow down', or 'free up', time, so that a new reality might be made visible, however fleetingly. I'll be happy if what we do just helps to create future memories of living on a council estate—"do you remember that summer when those back to the future people came to the estate?" While council estates like Middlefield Lane remain under threat today, we need to tread carefully and maybe accept that we do what we do as hopeful interventions only—and that any 'agency' or 'resilience' will always be located entirely within the subjectivity of the people who participate.

---

1 Chris Arnot, 'Art of the Matter', *The Guardian*, 13 August 2003.

2 Alison Ravetz, *Council Housing and Culture: The History of a Social Experiment*, London: Routledge, 2001, pp.5-6.

3 The Poly-Technic: poly-technic.co.uk

4 Owen Hatherley, *The Ministry of Nostalgia*, London: Verso, 2016, pp.201-202.

5 Felix Guattari, *The Three Ecologies*, London: Athlone Press, 2000, p.51.

MICHAEL GALLAGHER

Architecture about us

In the UK, the dominant attitude towards post-war modernist buildings has become a popular cliché: "concrete monstrosities, knock 'em down!" brutalism is perceived as brutality—a violence now directed back towards the buildings themselves. Tower block demolitions attract crowds of excited spectators, like public executions scaled up to the level of architecture. In some cases charity raffles have been held, with the lucky winner getting to press the button to detonate the explosives. It can seem as though mainstream society has collectively decided that this kind of architecture is unarguably worthless, that it must automatically be derided, like traffic, bad weather, or Simon Cowell.

This view is increasingly being challenged. There have been pro-brutalist polemics from commentators such as Owen Hatherley and Jonathan Meades. Architectural experts insist on the historical importance of post-war modernism. Campaigns for listing have been successful in some cases. Surprising levels of grassroots support have come out against the destruction of controversial modernist relics such as Preston Bus Station, the Apollo Pavilion and the Heygate Estate. With every high profile demolition, there is a growing sense of the value of what remains. Aesthetically, many of these buildings are uncompromising structures that stand out against the increasing blandness of contemporary cities. Historically, they are material remnants of the twentieth century. Politically they provide a connection to a worldview in which architecture was seen as a way to engineer better lives for people, rather than as a way of wringing profit from space, rebranding places or creating status symbols for cities.

It is important that any celebration of concrete heroics doesn't airbrush out the trickier details. Many modernist buildings were experimental, failing to function as intended. Some quickly became

Left: *The repetitive concrete of Edinburgh's St James Centre.*

grim places, usually due to a complex mix of factors. The uncompromising aesthetics of brutalist architecture can be intimidating, particularly in the UK, where damp climate and overcast skies turn concrete into a drab mass of rainy grey. Wet weather can infiltrate too, with flat roofs and experimental construction techniques being conducive to leaks. Such problems make a mockery of the masculinist rationalism underpinning architectural modernism, evident for instance in Le Corbusier's *Towards A New Architecture* with its eulogies to regulating lines and orderly plans.[1] That stance has since been blown apart—literally in many cases—by more wayward, ruinous forces.

Yet for all their shortcomings, post-war modernist buildings remain vital because they express a kind of anti-romantic honesty—a refreshing, sometimes shocking, brutal honesty—about the nature of modern life. Take the St James Centre, a shopping centre, hotel and ex-council office block in central Edinburgh. This grainy charcoal slab, looming over the edge of the city's genteel Georgian new town, is widely hated. As I write, its demolition is imminent, to make way for a shiny new development. It will likely have been reduced to rubble by the time this text is published. For the majority of Edinburgh residents, that will be cause for cheers not tears.

I am one of the few people who like this building. I have always found a mischievous joy in how it punctures the cosy heritage theme-park feel of Scotland's capital. Scraping against the veneer of a picturesque touristic landscape, it blocks scenic views from all directions. Its presence is audacious, almost to the point of being outright rude. In its final years, a giant redevelopment banner was hoisted across one of the most visible façades, like a loincloth trying to cover up an embarrassing erection—a desperate attempt to preserve modesty until the wrecking balls swing into action.

Scottish arts promoter Richard Demarco claimed that "no argument can defend the overscaled, heartless and meaningless modernism of the St James Centre development".[2] Well, here's my argument. Repetitive concrete structures such as the St James Centre act as in situ critiques of urban space, showing cities for what they really are: utilitarian, functional, impersonal places, where goods are traded and services provided. The St James Centre's affront to the bourgeois sensibilities of Edinburgh is reminiscent of the Greek cynic philosopher Diogenes defecating in public in Athens. His behaviour was not protest or exhibitionism but an attempt to cut through the bullshit of Athenian manners by living in a way that exposed the basic nature of human existence.

The St James Centre, awaiting demolition.

The St James Centre fire escape: impersonal infrastructure.

Buildings like the St James Centre are unavoidably modern, unashamedly over-rationalised. They don't pretend to be anything else. As a shopper, the space always left me in no doubt about exactly what I was in relation to it: an anonymous consumer. That direct, upfront quality can be attributed to post-war optimism, and a time when modern life was seen as the way forward, something to celebrate, to display with pride, not something to be ashamed of or hide away. Post-war modernist architecture openly expresses the incessantly repetitious, mass-mechanised character of late industrial societies, just as a thatched cottage in a rural village reflects something of the agrarian culture within which it was built.

There is a serious incongruity when people aspire to live in country manors or mock tudor houses, but spend their lives eating food produced by industrial farming, operating mass-produced machines, immersed in a haze of electromagnetic signals, all powered by fossil fuels extracted through heavy engineering. We can celebrate this way of life as bricolage, mash up, a post-modern merging of past and present, we can accept its inherent contradictions, or we can denigrate it as escapism, distraction and denial. Whatever position we take, the fact remains that much of the built environment conceals rather than reveals the structures and processes on which contemporary society is built. Dispirited by the violence of modernity, by its ravaging of life, we try to cover it up, or knock it down. In this situation, we need modernist architecture more than ever, in its successes and failures, in its rationality and madness, in renovation and in ruins, to help remind us of who, what, when and where we are.

....

1 Le Corbusier, *Towards a new architecture* [1931], Mineola, NY: Dover, 1986.

2 'Concrete monstrosities top ugly league', *The Scotsman*, 2002. scotsman.com/news/concrete-monstrosities-top-ugly-league-1-617669

Water Gardens, Harlow.

NATALIE BRADBURY

Bubbling away in the background—William Mitchell's Harlow fountains

The 1946 New Towns Act provided for eight new towns to be built around London, one of which was in Harlow, Essex. In preparation for submitting his plans for the New Town, Harlow's original architect, Frederick Gibberd, invested time in walking and cycling around the area. His vision was for a town centre built at the highest point of Harlow, surrounded by housing. Neighbourhoods would be grouped into four balanced districts, separated by greenery, so that everyone would live within walking distance of both shops and 'natural landscape'. Industry was to be situated separately, to the north of the town. Central to Harlow would be a civic centre and Italian-style piazza where public art could be seen and experienced. The Water Gardens, situated on a sloping site with stepped pools and formal gardens looking out onto an open green vista, were an important part of this vision.

Gibberd practised both landscape architecture and town planning, and Harlow's Water Gardens were intended to be an integral part of the landscaping of his post-war New Town. The prolific sculptor and designer William Mitchell, who worked with Gibberd in Harlow, observed in his autobiography that Gibberd "realised that infrastructure was required to give a sense of permanence and identity to new towns such as Harlow... Freddie insisted on features, such as water gardens and sculpture, so that it wasn't all roundabouts and dual carriageways."[1]

The situating of art around the town was accelerated by the formation of the Harlow Sculpture Trust in 1953. Writing about the work of the Trust, Gillian Whiteley observes that "sculpture soon became part of the fabric of Harlow", as part of a "1950s desire to combine social responsibility with modern architecture".[2] Sculptures by well-known British artists such as Lynn Chadwick, Henry Moore,

Barbara Hepworth and Elisabeth Frink moved out of the gallery and into the shopping areas and housing estates of Harlow, to be seen up close by the town's growing population (the birth rate of which was three times the national average in the 1950s, leading Harlow to be nicknamed 'pram town').

These sculptures might have been modern and in some cases abstract, but in many ways they still spoke the language of the institution, using traditional materials such as bronze and stone and standing on plinths. By contrast, William Mitchell's series of seven decorative fountainheads for the Water Gardens were both ornamental and functional, and form a colourful and playful intervention that is an integral part of their environment. Other artists such as Henry Moore might have made sculptures that were *placed in* housing estates and public spaces, but Mitchell made work that was *for* and *part of* these places, often in the form of sculptural reliefs and murals carefully designed both to beautify everyday environments and withstand the elements.

At the Water Gardens, Mitchell updates the gargoyle for the twentieth century using modern forms, techniques and materials. Cast in cement textured with exposed aggregate and inlaid mosaics, in the words of Mitchell they pour water from their mouths and eyes "as if crying with the sheer joy of being there". Mitchell was well aware that new towns and modern environments could appear severe and unwelcoming, and his gargoyles aimed to provide a human face to the town with designs that "were deliberately grotesque but not frighteningly so". The more you look, the more the fountainheads reveal. Fragmented creatures such as a lion and a whale emerge from Mitchell's jagged and interweaving shapes: an eye here, an eyelash there, an eyebrow, a foot, scales, a nose. Mitchell hoped that "small children could relate, for example, 'to the one with the big eyes', or the boat, on which you could sail away to a better school".

Like many of Mitchell's other prominent post-war commissions, such as his 'Minute Men' figures outside the University of Salford, the fountains incorporate Aztec influences. Where they survive these striking interventions are increasingly recognised by heritage bodies for their contribution to both the buildings and wider areas in which they are situated, and for the way in which they bring a touch of the exotic to a functional urban environment. The 'Minute Men' are among ten of Mitchell's works to have been listed in recent years (including those at Harlow), for the "distinct identity and image" they bring to the campus. The most recent listing of Mitchell's work is his imposing, sheep-centred mural for the International Wool Secretariat

Mitchell gargoyles.

Heraldic Panel.

in Ilkley, West Yorkshire, which was one of 41 sculptures to receive listed status in January 2016, as part of a Historic England focus on recognising the artworks which were "designed to bring our public spaces back to life after WWII".

Alongside his gargoyles, two other pieces by Mitchell were commissioned in Harlow. 'Heraldic Panel' is a smooth sculptural relief, originally situated on the Town Hall which stood alongside the Water Gardens. Mitchell also created a patterned concrete relief for the Civic Square. Though Grade II listed, by the turn of the twenty first century it was feared that the Water Gardens could be lost to make way for regeneration of the area. In 2003, Gibberd's landmark Town Hall, with its tall clock tower, was demolished and replaced with a brand new civic centre surrounded by a large supermarket, chain clothes shops and restaurants. The development retained the name the 'Water Gardens', though both the name and the area became synonymous with retail. Rather than being removed and demolished Mitchell's panel and relief were reinstalled, albeit in somewhat undignified fashion, on the exterior walls of commercial buildings. In an interview in 2011 Mitchell told me of his frustration with post-war artworks that were "thought of as brooches to stick on the building"

rather than conceived of as part of a complete environment. Today, however, his Town Hall relief can be found attached to the greying panels of an Asda supermarket, astride a large roundabout and busy dual carriageway, and his 'Heraldic Panel' is hidden high-up in an unglamorous pedestrian passageway facing onto a back entrance for a now defunct British Home Stores.

It is not uncommon for artworks commissioned for public places to be removed, relocated—or forgotten about altogether—as the places in which they are situated age, and fashions change. A mid-century pedestrianised shopping precinct or a landscaped social housing estate that looks clean, light, functional and airy in planners' documents and architects' models may look bleak, empty, and tired fifty years later when the aesthetic and social ideals behind it have faded or been replaced by a new set of values. A sculpture or mural placed outside a tower block or in a municipal library with the best of intentions, as a way of decorating an otherwise plain space, conferring prestige and democratising culture, might never be taken to heart by the space's users, or appear strange, dated and ugly. Though held in esteem by those who commissioned them, artworks of these kind (which are often abstract) might have no obvious use and value to those who walk past them everyday day. By their twenty-first century successors in town halls and planning departments, meanwhile, they can be regarded as a luxury, an add-on to the functional obligations of a place or, if the artist happens to be famous, as an excuse to raise some funds through an auction sale.

In 2015, Historic England launched a public campaign to 'Help Find Our Missing Art', which highlighted the various pitfalls which have befallen public artworks, from being stolen and vandalised, to lack of maintenance, being lost, sold, moved or destroyed to make way for redevelopment. These are some of the fates which have met several of Mitchell's plethora of post-war commmissions: a large, round, spiky sculpture nicknamed 'the Pineapple', which once stood in the centre of another Essex new town, Basildon, appears to have been misplaced since its removal to storage by its owner in 2011 when redevelopment was planned for the area. In Hatfield, a new town in the neighbouring county of Hertfordshire, a huge sculptural panel designed for the Lee Valley Water Company has recently been reinstated on the side wall of a new-build block of Barratt flats. The end result appears absurdly out-of-place—especially so since the post-war trend for aesthetically and culturally elevating new public housing with murals and sculptural commissions has now been consigned to a different time. The humdrum blandness of the Barratt build ensures it looks like any of hundreds of other private sector housing developments across the country, whereas Mitchell's jagged, layered shapes command attention from the eye and can't help but arouse interest and surprise in the viewer. Large by any scale, Mitchell's panel appears outlandishly oversized in the setting of a domestic estate.

In Harlow, the town council is more proud than most to promote the role of public art dating from the post-war period in the town's heritage and ongoing cultural offer. In 2009, the council voted to rebrand Harlow as 'Sculpture Town'. Early in 2016, Historic England's exhibition 'Out There: Our Post-War Public Art', held at Somerset House in London, dedicated a large section to Harlow's collection, its ethos and the part it played in shaping the town's identity. Mitchell's gargoyles and reliefs can be found, along with the rest of the extensive collection, on a Harlow Sculpture Map that is freely available from the civic centre. The map identifies trails around the town for the sculpture-seeking visitor, thereby reinforcing Harlow's identity as 'Sculpture Town'.

When I visited, on a grey, stormy day in early April, the landscaped area of the Water Gardens was populated by nesting birds, lunching office workers, small children out shopping with their parents, and young people loitering for a drink and a smoke. However, the Water Gardens brand is now owned by the investment company Standard Life: the public and civic functions of Gibberd's original ideals for the Water Gardens have been overtaken by private and commercial interests. Bubbling away gently in the background, as his only Harlow artworks to remain in their original location while the town has changed around them, Mitchell's Water Gardens gargoyles are a reminder of the transformation which both Harlow and British society have undergone over the past sixty years. Despite the seemingly irreversible shift from the cultural, political and social aspirations of the post-war welfare state to a society dominated by neoliberal ideology, Mitchell's Harlow fountains remain part of a distinctive urban environment that came to pioneer and symbolise new ways of living, working, socialising and encountering culture.

1 William Mitchell, *Self Portrait: The Eyes Within*, Whittles Publishing, 2013.
2 Gillian Whiteley, *Sculpture in Harlow*, Harlow Sculpture Trust, 2005.

Park Hill New and Old.

JOHN PENDLEBURY & AIDAN WHILE

Post-war social housing: conservation and regeneration

One dimension of the planning system that has assumed considerable significance over the last half century is conservation-planning; the legislation and policy that seeks to identify important historic buildings and environments and to protect them over time. But as a goal of public policy, conservation-planning exists in tandem with other public policy objectives. These include physical, social and economic regeneration goals. In this chapter we consider these connected issues with respect to the heritage of post-war social housing in England. In the next section we further discuss conservation-planning and the politics of urban change, before shifting our focus more directly to the heritage of modernism.

Conservation planning and the politics of urban change

The conservation-planning protection regime defines heritage in various legally-defined categories (most significantly 'listed buildings'—our focus here—and 'conservation areas'), with government policy then identifying the importance of protection in the management of urban change. In practice the British conservation-planning system, and the listing system in particular, hinge largely on the notion of 'special architectural or historic interest', which privileges a particular way of constructing heritage around age value and the value of the architectural canon—buildings that are very old or are considered of architectural quality and probably designed by recognised architects. In managing change the goal of heritage professionals will usually be to protect the historic fabric or the aesthetic qualities of the building.

However, in the management of the urban environment the conservation-planning system is sometimes in competition with other elite interests expressed as forces of change, whether in terms of capital accumulation or other social policy goals, such as economic and social regeneration. One of the great successes of the conservation movement has been to reposition conservation from being understood as a *barrier* to change to being accepted as an *agent* of change. This is a process given initial impetus in 1979 with the election of a Conservative government looking for market-orientated, instrumental approaches across a broad swath of the public sector. Over the following decades the historic environment sector succeeded in not only defending its sphere of activity, but in extending its reach and policy significance, due in part to the sector's success in positioning itself as complementary to economic growth and physical regeneration. The election of a Labour Government in 1997 posed new challenges, with social inclusion a powerful rhetoric adopted across the cultural sector as a matter of necessity and expediency. It is within this context of heritage acquiring new instrumental roles that we need to examine the listing and conservation of post-war social housing.

Listing post-war social housing

From the 1980s onwards there was growing momentum from English Heritage (now Historic England) and architectural elites to extend the system of listed building protection to buildings constructed after 1945. The listing of post-war modernism in its various forms was controversial and most of English Heritage's initial recommendations for listing were turned down by government. Public housing presented particular challenges given the decades of widespread vilification such architecture had received. Ushered in as a central component of the welfare state, architectural innovation was used in the challenge of improving living conditions for the working class and, alongside schools, housing was the central area of innovation in architectural design. However, since the 1970s modernist social housing had been submerged in a blanket critique from the political Left and Right for its technical and social failings and stood accused of creating dehumanising living environments that fractured previously tight-knit and vibrant communities. Modernist estates were characterised by crime and anti-social behaviour reflecting the lack of 'defensible space' and the loss of traditional street patterns.[1] Much was made of the technical failings of experimental building types, particularly after the partial collapse of the Ronan Point tower block in east London following a gas explosion in 1968, with the death of four residents. This came to be seen as a period of architecture and planning that had produced buildings that were not just temporarily unpopular and out-of-step with contemporary design principles, but that produced environments contributing to urban decline and social breakdown.

Nevertheless, in 1993 the Alexandra Road Estate (Camden Architects' Department, North London) and Keeling House (Denys Lasdun, East London) were the first post-war council housing projects to be listed and a significant number of estates were listed by the new Labour government in 1998. Whilst the success of English Heritage in building political support for the protection of post-war social housing has subsequently waxed and waned, nevertheless, significant numbers of post-war housing estates have now been listed on grounds of architectural or historic significance, with a heavy concentration in London. This is listing by exception; the estates listed are the architectural one-offs, generally by well-known architects, rather than the typical system-built housing of the period. The blanket critique of post-war social housing ignores the empirical reality that often such estates have continued to provide good quality affordable housing. Equally, however, it is important to recognise that many such estates, including some of those listed, face multiple problems in continuing to function as viable and sustainable social housing. Estates, now approaching or over half a century old, were often built with new materials and technologies that have not always stood the test of time. Many estates have suffered from years of under investment and their stigmatization as residual social housing. Thus there can be design and technical failings or wider social and economic problems not specific to the particular estate but a wider locale, or very often a mixture of the two. Problems can be addressed through regeneration and investment. But regeneration projects can have very different goals, depending upon what combination of physical, social and economic objectives are prioritised. In the next part of the chapter we focus on three brief examples of listed estates involved in regeneration projects and the very different outcomes that have arisen.

Conservation through radical physical and social transformation

Park Hill in Sheffield (see p.126) was listed in the knowledge that the estate needed major intervention if its future was to be secured.

This substantial, pioneering late-1950s deck-access council housing scheme, designed by the young architects Jack Lynn and Ivor Smith in the City Council Architect's Office, sits in a prominent location overlooking the city centre. Listed in 1998, this was always a controversial and problematic listing, bitterly opposed by some locally, given not only the general unpopularity of such buildings but also the poor physical condition of the estate, combined with major social problems. Initially the conservation strategy for the estate's regeneration focused upon upgrading the fabric with the tenure of the estate unchanged. However, the scale of the physical and social problems combined with a lack of available finance to invest in social housing ultimately led to a very different approach. Park Hill was handed over to the developers Urban Splash together with substantial public resource to achieve regeneration, a process slowed by the 2008 crash. Urban Splash are implementing a mixed scheme that retains some social housing but is predominantly owner occupation. Furthermore, to facilitate something happening, English Heritage took a controversially radical view of how much change was permissible to the fabric of Park Hill to enable its reuse. The flats were stripped back to the concrete frame, justified by English Heritage as the heritage values were deemed to lie

> "not only in the site's history but in the scale and vision of the original council housing scheme, in the expressed reinforced concrete frame and the relationship of the building to the landscape in which it sits. Substantial changes to the internal layout and the infill panels within the frame could therefore be introduced without damaging its historic significance."[2]

Thus Park Hill is being largely appropriated for owner occupied housing and materially radically changed in the process.

Conservation through planned gentrification

Balfron Tower (opposite) is a 26 storey residential tower containing 146 flats and a part of the Brownfields Estate in east London. It was designed by architect Ernö Goldfinger in 1963 for London County Council alongside the lower, adjacent listed Carradale House. In 2007 residents of the Brownfields Estate voted for the stock transfer of the estate from Tower Hamlets to the housing association Poplar

Right: *Balfron Tower.*

HARCA, with the incentive of promised property upgrades. Balfron Tower residents were told they could choose to remain in situ during refurbishment works or be rehoused elsewhere. Ultimately, however, Poplar HARCA determined the scale of the block overhaul would require a total decant on safety grounds and at this point the fate of the residents wanting to remain became much more ambiguous with Poplar HARCA finally concluding displaced residents could not return. Poplar HARCA's strategy has become one of refurbishment for sale. It has entered in a partnership with a joint venture company United House Developments and luxury residential property development company Londonewcastle, whose website states

> "…more and more opportunities begin in the public sector. A new world needs a new kind of developer, one who unlocks the potential for an unprecedented cast of stakeholders and also for the places it seeks to change."[3]

Applied to Balfron, this suggests a quality of design that needs unlocking and exploiting in a new way. This view of the benefits of changing tenure can also be found in the architecture world: Peter Murray, architecture writer and chairman of New London Architecture told *Time Out*,

> "I think as long as other accommodation is provided in the area, it does often mean that these pieces of architecture are looked after rather better when they have private owners."[4]

Balfron will no longer be social housing and the promises made to residents in 2007 have been reneged on. In the case of Balfron Tower the message is clear; these flats are now too valuable for social housing.

Conservation as progressive practice?

At the time of its construction the Byker estate (opposite) in Newcastle-upon-Tyne was celebrated nationally and internationally for its architectural design and its novel processes of engaging with residents. Architect Ralph Erskine set up office in the heart of the area with an open door policy and residents were encouraged to drop in, to talk to the architects and see the emerging proposals. Architecturally, concrete and brutalism were replaced by light

Left: *Byker: High and low-rise.*

materials such as timber cladding and metal roofs, often brightly coloured. The northern edge of the estate is defined by a variable height tall perimeter block, the so-called Byker Wall, which snakes along the top of a steep slope. The rest of the estate, falling steeply down the hill, is low rise, comprising over 1600 houses, maisonettes and flats of various sizes. Cars were mostly kept at the periphery of the estate and some older buildings such as churches and pubs were retained. Dwellings were pre-allocated with a strong concern for facilitating the retention of neighbourly contacts that were seen to be supportive, although ultimately less than half of the old Byker residents returned.

Like many working class districts, Byker was hit hard in the 1980s by industrial decline and at the same time council budgets for housing and grounds maintenance budgets were slashed; always an issue with Byker and its 'light' materials and its abundant public greenspace. Anti-social behaviour, vacancy and vandalism became a problem in parts of the Estate. These problems reached crisis point in the late 1990s, when the local authority proposed the demolition of an area called Bolam Coyne, together with some adjacent terraces. In response a campaign developed to have the estate listed, supported by an English Heritage recommendation in 2000 and, eventually, in 2007 the entirety of the Erskine Byker estate was listed.

Subsequently the conjunction of the estate's listing, and the different and more expensive management approaches this might require, together with a strong tradition of community infrastructure, led a commission created by the government, the city council and the Homes and Communities Agency to recommend the passing of ownership of the estate to a mutual community trust; effectively therefore from the City Council to residents. Following a vote in favour of the proposals by Byker residents, the stock transferred to the Byker Community Trust in July 2012. Investment in the housing and the wider estate has proceeded apace, including the renovation of the longstanding sore of Bolam Coyne, subsequently winning regeneration and design awards. In the case of Byker, listing has triggered governance and funding changes and opportunities enabling regeneration and conservation to go hand in hand, for the benefit of existing residents.

*

Listing can be criticised as elitist imposition if it imposes costs on social housing tenants and local authorities and becomes an obstacle to much needed regeneration. Conversely, the post-war listing programme has also been criticised for facilitating the gentrification of social housing by generating a heritage premium that attracts private developers. In the case of Park Hill the cost of regeneration combined with the low political priority of investing in social housing led to a radical transformation of the fabric and a major shift in tenure pattern from social renting to owner occupation. With Balfron Tower the cost of repair combined with the super-heated London property market lead to the conclusion that Balfron is too valuable to be put to its original purpose; better to sell its design qualities to a more affluent demographic and use the receipts to meet social housing obligations of rehousing displaced tenants, presumably in less generous apartments.

Thus post-war listing is simultaneously protecting the legacies of welfare state modernism and is part of the erosion of this legacy. Heritage-led gentrification suggests that it was the principle of social housing that failed rather than the architecture, with some commentators concluding that the design qualities are wasted on tenants and gentrification generates a better heritage solution. The revalorisation of post-war listing is linked to a wider process of austerity nostalgia in which post-war design and architecture is fetishised at a time when the underlying principles of the welfare state are under attack.[5] Architecture is rehabilitated, whilst the idea of council housing is further diminished as part of a steady and stigmatised residualisation.

The primary cause of the processes we describe is not listing. Rather, it relates to deeper shifts in tenure patterns and access to housing, facilitated through political ideology and housing policy. We see embedded ideas of regeneration equating to maximising economic value. But the existence of conservation status does have an agency and plays an important role in shaping possible outcomes in each case. Were it not for listing, Park Hill would probably have been demolished. The resultant building continues as a dominant element in the landscape but is far removed from the architectural form and the social purpose of the original. Listing has opened up the possibility of valorising and re-positioning Balfron Tower for middle class consumption as an icon of retro-modern living, in the process creating an all too visible slap in the face for the welfare state ideals that underpinned the building's production. Only at Byker has regeneration not been about demolition and gentrification. Far removed from the pressure cooker of London and with a different institutional and social milieu or indeed the city centre site of Park Hill, the listing process has been used as a springboard for a more creative solution to addressing the estate's problems. In Byker innovation is supporting a renewal of the ideals of the original formation of the Estate; providing good housing, and a decent neighbourly environment as a public good. Ironically, national protection has led to a path whereby ownership, management and control of resources have become more local and seem to have created a context whereby a regeneration of the estate for its existing residents has been enabled.

1 Oscar Newman, *Defensible space: crime prevention through urban design*, London: Macmillan, 1972. See also Alice Coleman, *Utopia on Trial: Vision and Reality in Planned Housing*, London: Hilary Shipman, 1990.

2 English Heritage, *Constructive Conservation in Practice*, London: English Heritage, 2008, 44. p.14.

3 londonewcastle.com viewed 9 July 2016.

4 timeout.com/london/things-to-do/the-changing-fortunes-of-balfron-tower viewed 9 July 2016.

5 Owen Hatherley, *The Ministry of Nostalgia*, London: Verso, 2016.

MODERN FUTURES

Contributors

IAIN ANDERSON is an Architecture Survey Project Manager at Historic Environment Scotland.

NATALIE BRADBURY is a researcher, currently working on Pictures for Schools, a series of post-war exhibitions aimed at getting original works of art into schools.

RICHARD BROOK is a Principal Lecturer in Architecture at the Manchester School of Architecture.

ANGELA CONNELLY is a researcher at the University of Manchester.

RUTH CRAGGS is a Lecturer in Cultural and Historical Geography at King's College, London.

MICHAEL GALLAGHER is a Research Fellow in the Faculty of Education at Manchester Metropolitan University.

ESTHER JOHNSON is an artist and filmmaker, and Reader in Media Arts at Sheffield Hallam University.

VERITY-JANE KEEFE is a visual artist working predominantly in the public realm to explore the complex relationship between people and place.

ANDY LOCK is an artist and researcher who works with photography. He is currently based at Bergen Academy of Art and Design.

HANNAH NEATE is a Lecturer in Human Geography at Manchester Metropolitan University.

JOHN PENDLEBURY is a Professor of Urban Conservation at Newcastle University. He is a town planner and urban conservationist.

EDDY RHEAD is a founding trustee of the Manchester Modernist Society.

MATTHEW STEELE is a Manchester-based researcher and writer on architecture and urbanism.

SALLY STONE is a Reader at the Manchester School of Architecture.

IAN WAITES is a Senior Lecturer in History of Art and Design at the University of Lincoln.

CHRISTINE WALL is a Reader at the University of Westminster where she is Co-Director of the Centre for Research into the Production of the Built Environment (ProBE).

AIDAN WHILE is a Senior Lecturer in the Department of Urban Studies and Planning at the University of Sheffield.

MATTHEW WHITFIELD is an Architectural Investigator at Historic England.

MODERN FUTURES

Photographic credits

Introduction p.8 Michael Gallagher. *"You'd concrete and say a wee prayer"—the South Bank Arts Complex and new notions of value in modern architecture* p.16, p.18, pp.21–22 Rod Bond. *Mid-Century Modern Living* p.26, pp.29–34 Esther Johnson. *Mainstream Modern* p.36, pp.39–40, p.42, p.45 Richard Brook. *The Suburbs Project* p.46, pp.49–50, p.53 Matthew Whitfield. *Surveying Greater Manchester's Sacred Suburbs* p.56 Matthew Steele, p.60 Paterson Macaulay & Owens, p.63 Jack Hale, p.64 Eccles Congregational Church. *The use of photography in recording the legacy of the modern movement in Britain's post-war landscapes* p.66, p.68 Andy Lock, p.70 above Crown Copyright: Historic Environment Scotland, p.70 below Andy Lock, p.72 D. M. Hall LLP, p.73 above Crown Copyright: Historic Environment Scotland, p.73 below Andy Lock. *From Here to Modernity—Manchester Modernist Society* pp.76–77, pp.79–80, p.83 Jack Hale. *Gate 81* p.84, pp.87–91 Sally Stone. *The Mobile Museum* p.92, pp.94–96, pp.99–100 Verity-Jane Keefe. *'Spontaneous Estate Evolution'—Research/Practice interventions on a 1960s council estate* p.102 Ian Waites, pp.104–105 Gainsborough Heritage Association, pp.107–108 Ian Waites. *Architecture about us* p.112, pp.115–116 Michael Gallagher. *Bubbling away in the background—William Mitchell's Harlow fountains* p.118, pp.121–123 Natalie Bradbury. *Post-war social housing: conservation and regeneration* p.126, pp.131–132 John Pendlebury.

This book draws on a series of workshops and discussions supported by the Arts and Humanities Research Council (ref: AH/L015323/1) and Manchester Metropolitan University.